farlaine the goblin

by Pug Grumble

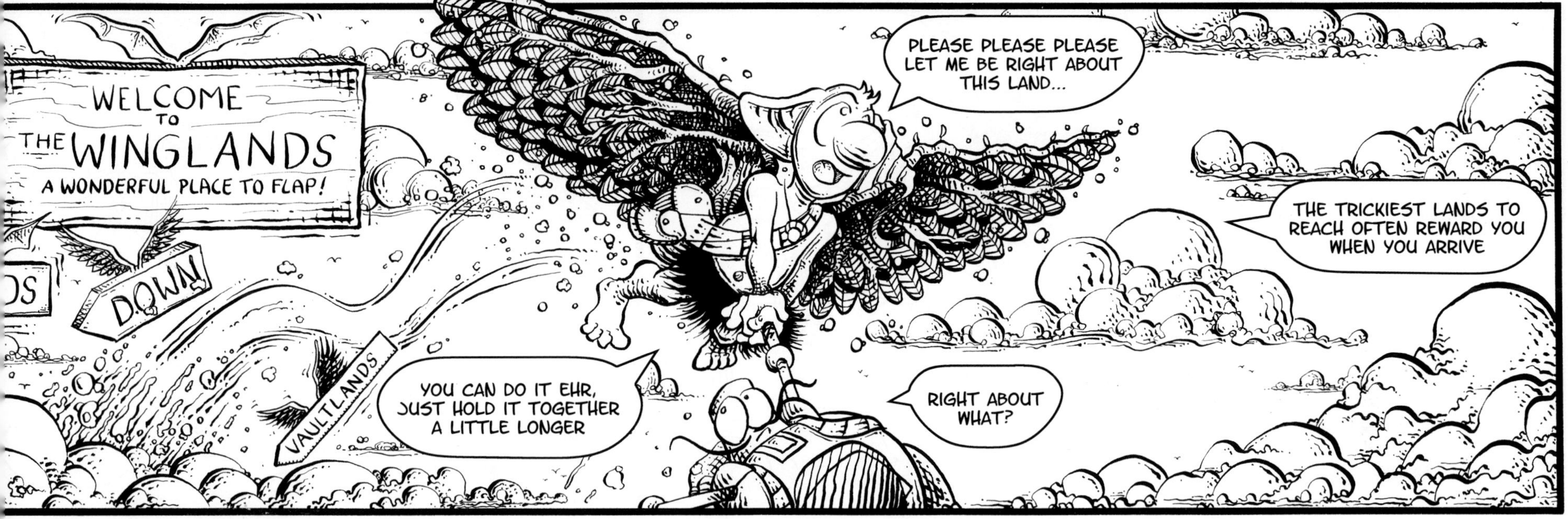
WELCOME TO THE WINGLANDS
A WONDERFUL PLACE TO FLAP!
DS
DOWN
VAULTLANDS
PLEASE PLEASE PLEASE LET ME BE RIGHT ABOUT THIS LAND...
THE TRICKIEST LANDS TO REACH OFTEN REWARD YOU WHEN YOU ARRIVE
YOU CAN DO IT EHR, JUST HOLD IT TOGETHER A LITTLE LONGER
RIGHT ABOUT WHAT?

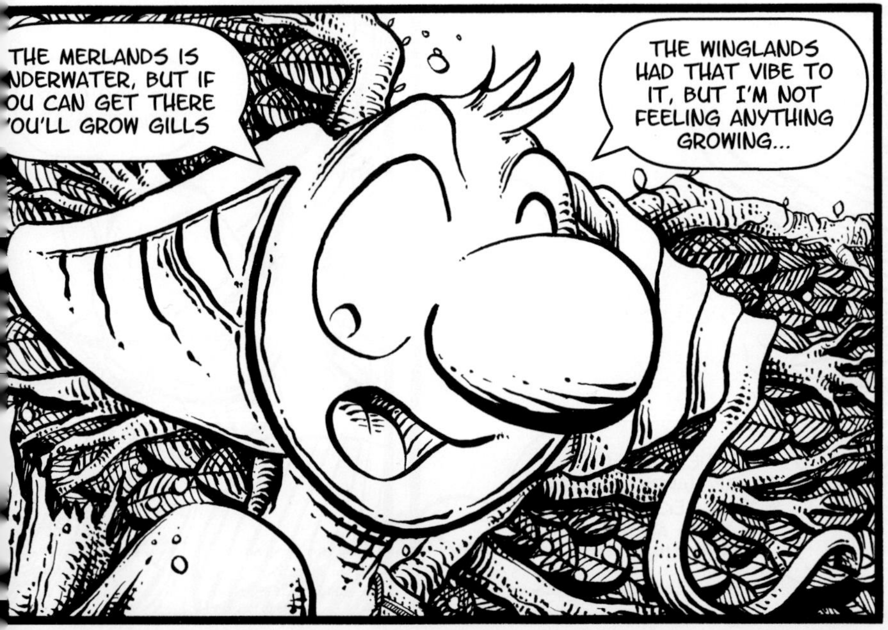
THE MERLANDS IS NDERWATER, BUT IF OU CAN GET THERE OU'LL GROW GILLS
THE WINGLANDS HAD THAT VIBE TO IT, BUT I'M NOT FEELING ANYTHING GROWING...

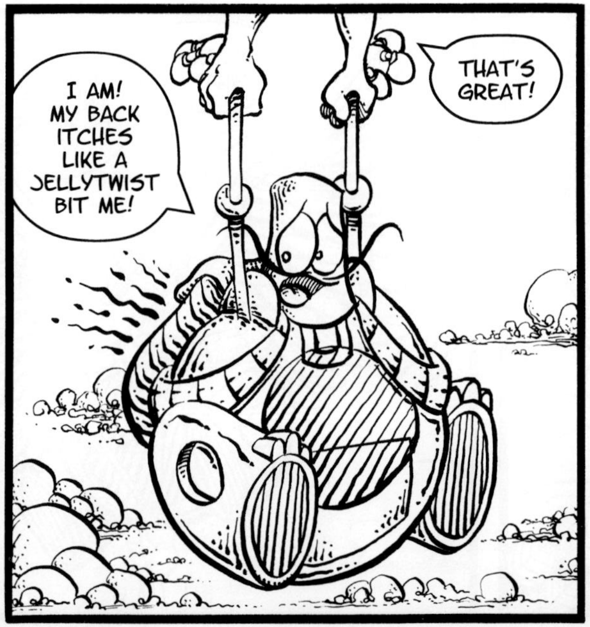
I AM! MY BACK ITCHES LIKE A JELLYTWIST BIT ME!
THAT'S GREAT!

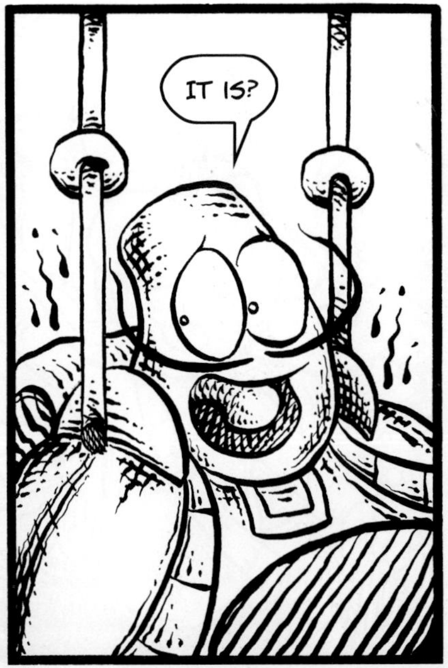
IT IS?

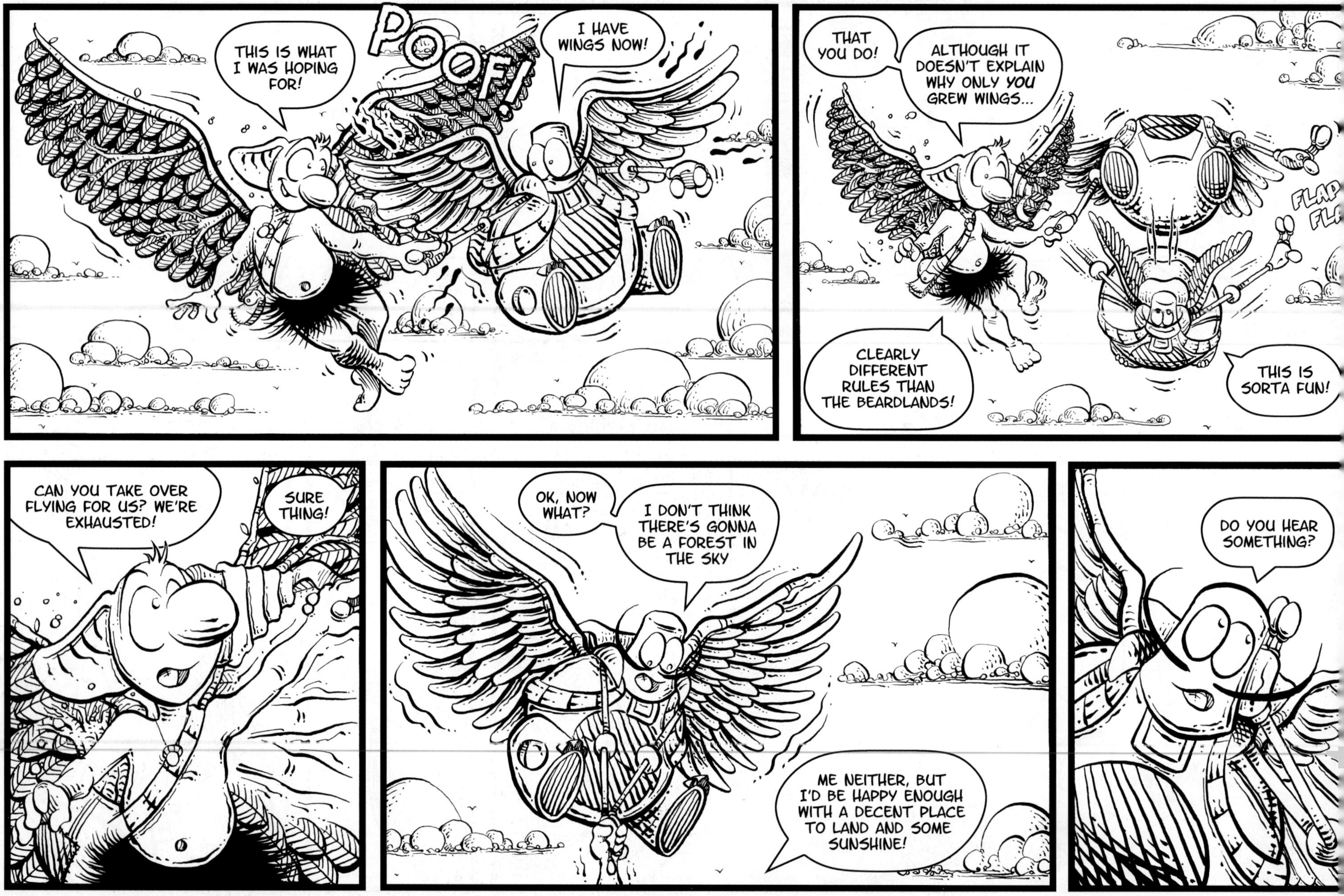
THIS IS WHAT I WAS HOPING FOR!
POOF!
I HAVE WINGS NOW!
THAT YOU DO!
ALTHOUGH IT DOESN'T EXPLAIN WHY ONLY YOU GREW WINGS...
CLEARLY DIFFERENT RULES THAN THE BEARDLANDS!
THIS IS SORTA FUN!
CAN YOU TAKE OVER FLYING FOR US? WE'RE EXHAUSTED!
SURE THING!
OK, NOW WHAT?
I DON'T THINK THERE'S GONNA BE A FOREST IN THE SKY
ME NEITHER, BUT I'D BE HAPPY ENOUGH WITH A DECENT PLACE TO LAND AND SOME SUNSHINE!
DO YOU HEAR SOMETHING?

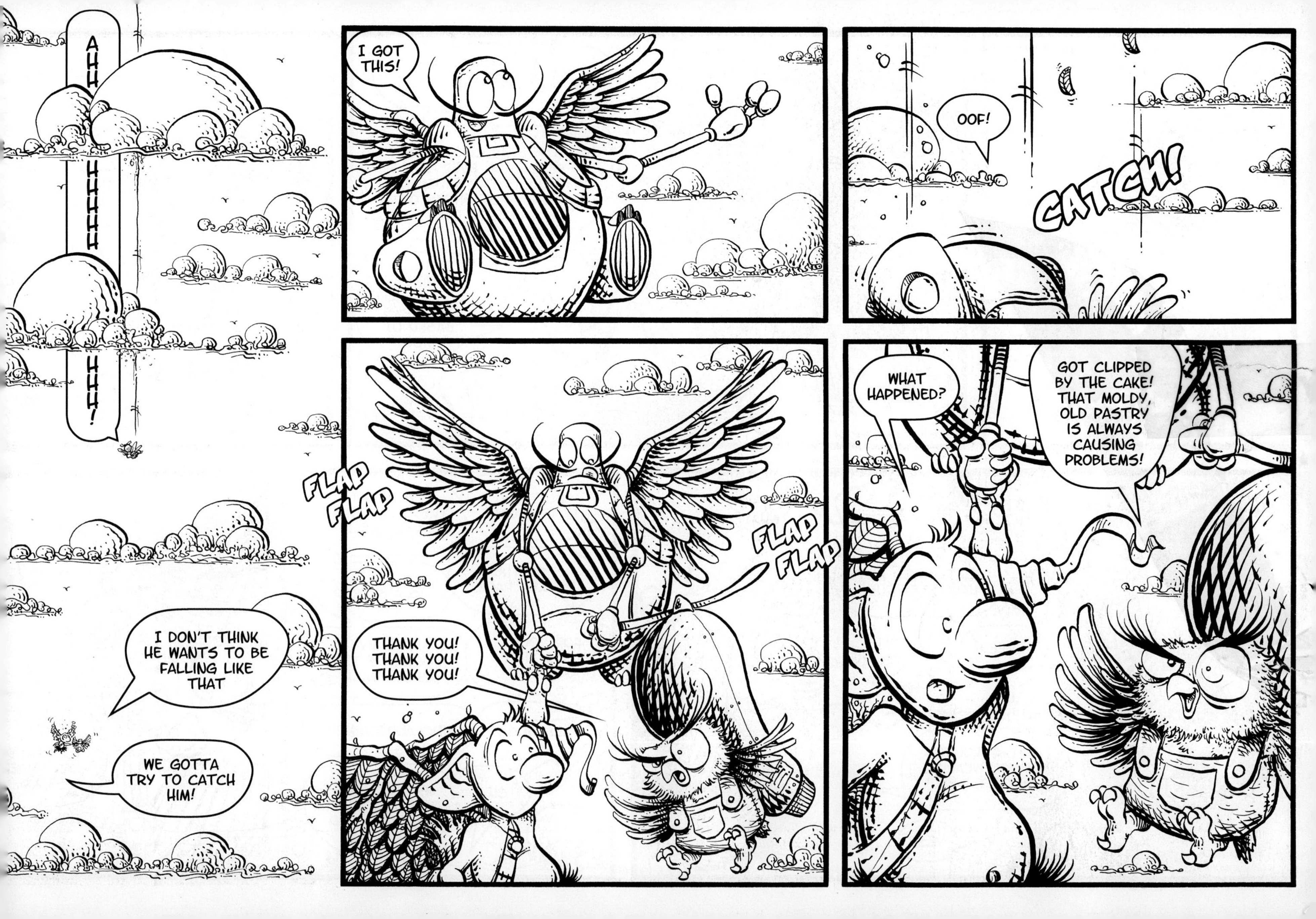
AHHHHHHHHHHHH!
I DON'T THINK HE WANTS TO BE FALLING LIKE THAT
WE GOTTA TRY TO CATCH HIM!
I GOT THIS!
OOF!
CATCH!
FLAP FLAP
FLAP FLAP
THANK YOU! THANK YOU! THANK YOU!
WHAT HAPPENED?
GOT CLIPPED BY THE CAKE! THAT MOLDY, OLD PASTRY IS ALWAYS CAUSING PROBLEMS!

LUCKILY YOU'RE BIGGER THAN ME OR I WOULDA STOLEN YOUR WINGS!
AHHHH, THAT EXPLAINS IT!
WHAT EXPLAINS WHAT?
GROWTH LANDS LIKE THIS CAN WORK DIFFERENT WAYS
THE BEARDLANDS GREW BEARDS ON EVERYTHING, WHEREAS THE SHOELANDS ONLY PUT SHOES ON UNSHOD FEET
THE WINGANDS SOUNDS LIKE IT WORKS BASED ON SIZE!
SIZE?
IF TWO THINGS ARE TOUCHING, ONL THE BIGGEST GET THE WINGS!
WHICH EXPLAINS WH I GREW WING INSTEAD OF YOU!
EXACTLY!
...AND WHY IF YOU WERE SMALLER YOU WOULDA LOST YOUR WINGS INSTEAD OF ME!
THAT WOULD NOT HAVE BEEN FUN!
AGREED!
WAIT A MINUTE, ARE YOU WEARING A ROCKET PACK?
YES?
BUT...YOU HAVE WINGS?
YES, BUT THEY DON'T WORK VERY WELL
SO THE ROCKET PACK...
...IS A BACKUP
FOR YOUR WINGS THAT DON'T WORK...
FOR MY WINGWINGS THAT MAY VANISH
WINGWINGS?
WINGLANDS WINGS
OH...
MY REAL WINGS ARE JUST FOR PLUMAGE AND PRANCING
ONE DAY HOPE WE TO A LAND CAN UNDE STAND...

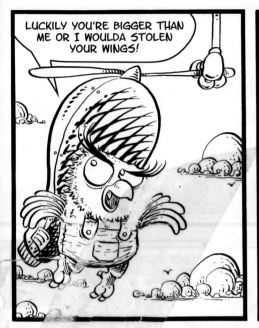

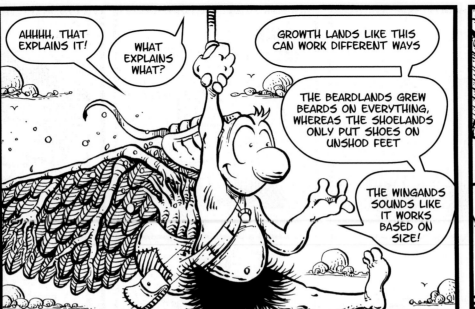

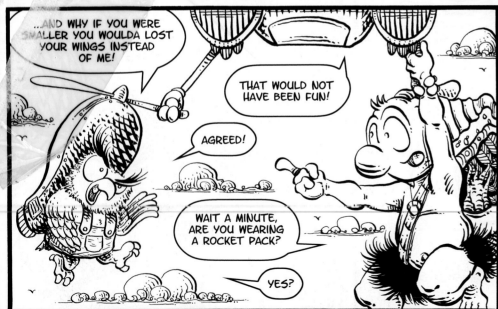

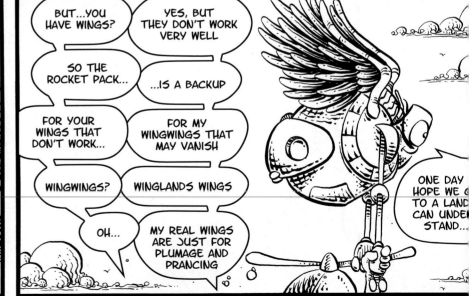

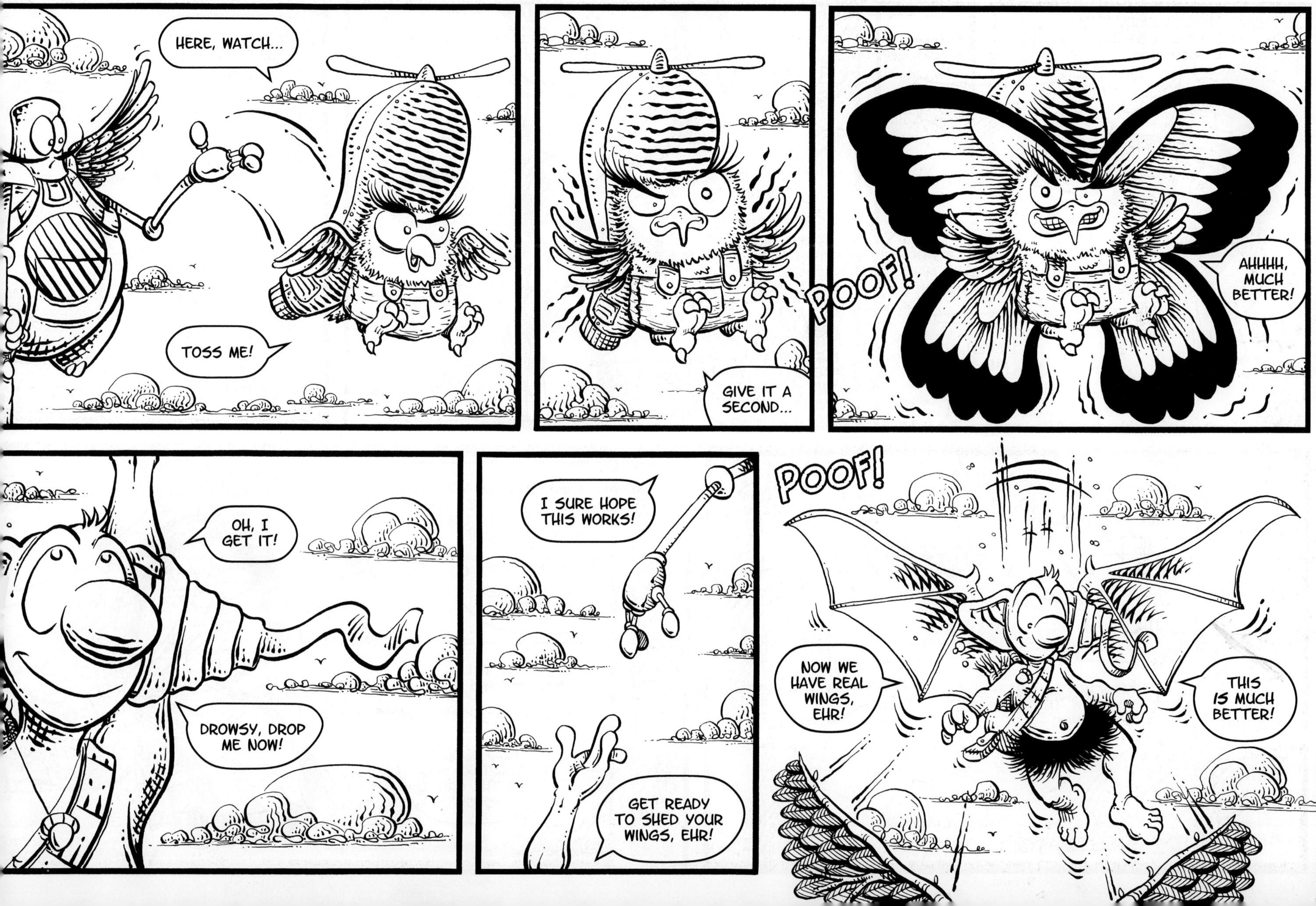
HERE, WATCH...
TOSS ME!
GIVE IT A SECOND...
POOF!
AHHHH, MUCH BETTER!
OH, I GET IT!
DROWSY, DROP ME NOW!
I SURE HOPE THIS WORKS!
GET READY TO SHED YOUR WINGS, EHR!
POOF!
NOW WE HAVE REAL WINGS, EHR!
THIS IS MUCH BETTER!

BUT WHY DID WE ALL GROW DIFFERENT KINDS OF WINGS?
THE LAWS OF THE LAND MAKE IT RANDOM!
I EVEN GREW PIG-WINGS ONCE...
I'M BEXBY BY THE WAY
A PLEASURE TO MEET YOU!
I'M FARLAINE, THE SHRUB IS EHRENWORT, AND THE FELLOW WITH THE WASHBOARD AB IS DROWSY!
SO I TAKE IT YOU JUST ARRIVED HERE?
YUP! WE CAME UP FROM THE VAULTLANDS
WELCOME! THE FIRST THING YOU FOLKS ARE GONNA NEED ARE CHUTES!
WHEN YOU SAY 'CHUTES' YOU MEAN...
PARACHUTES! YA KNOW, IN CASE YOU FALL
WINGWINGS VANISH WHEN YOU LEAVE THE WINGLANDS...BEST BE PREPARED TO HAVE A WAY TO LAND WITHOUT THEM!
I WENT WITH A ROCKET PACK MYSELF...
SEEMED MORE FUN AT THE TIME, BUT SADLY BREAKS DOWN QUITE OFTEN...
FLAP ALONG, I'LL TAKE YOU TO THE CHUTE SHOP!

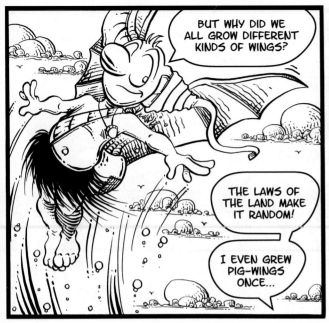

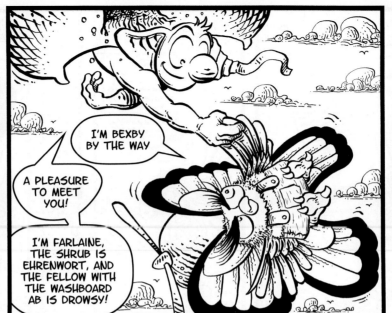

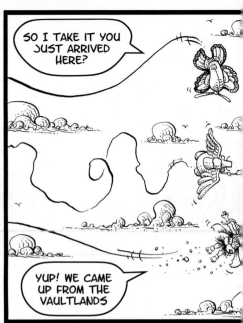

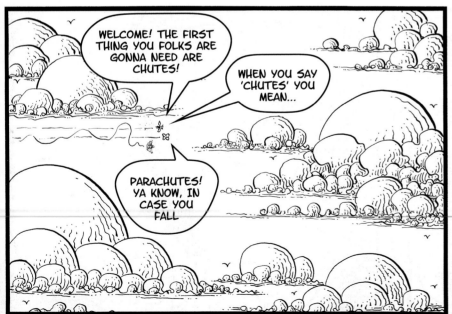

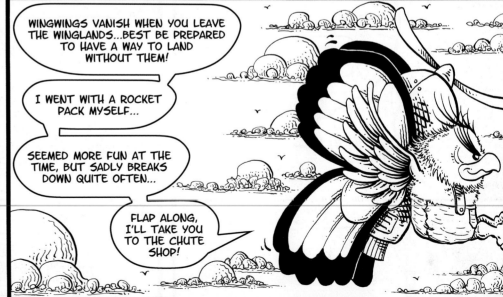

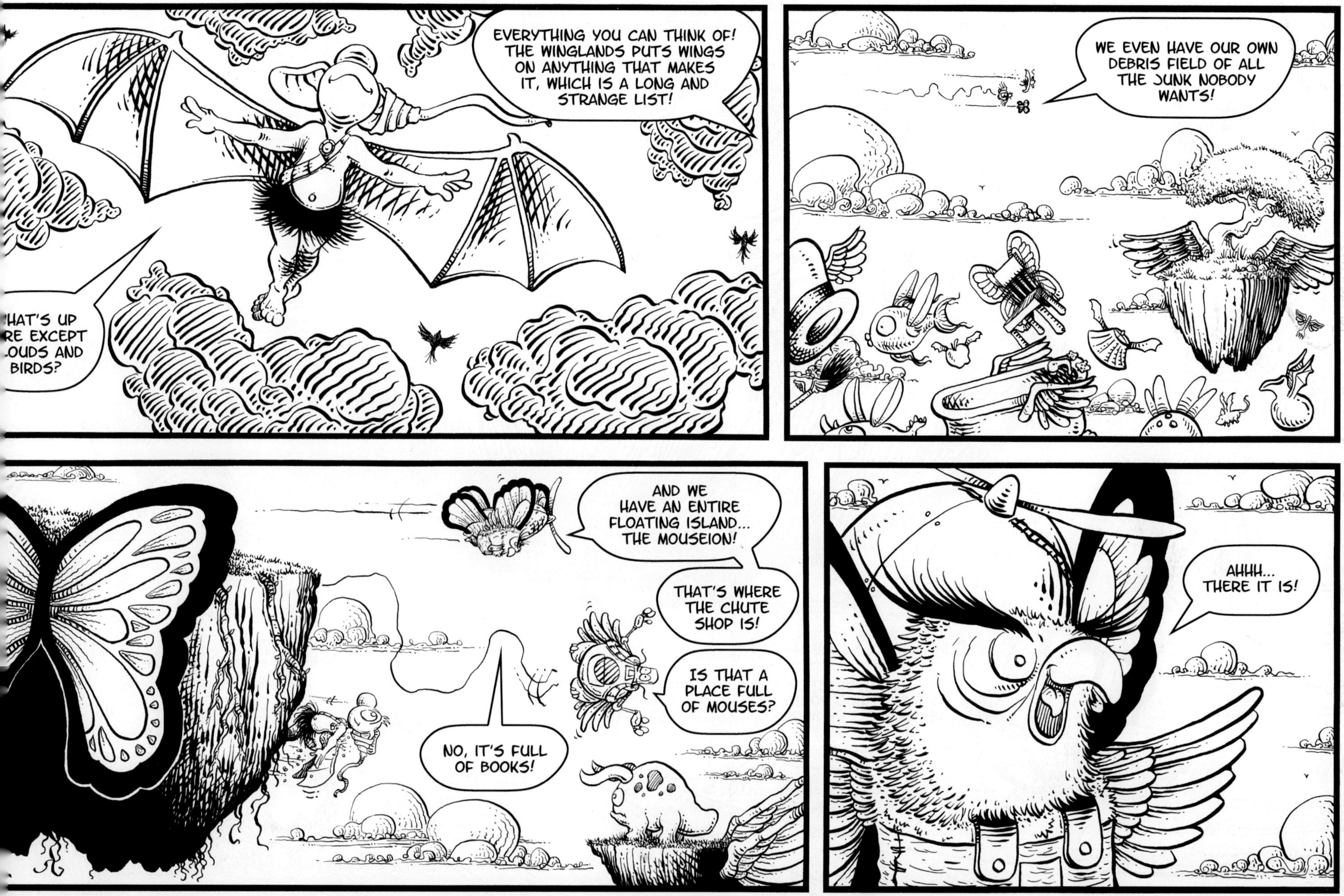

HAT'S UP RE EXCEPT LOUDS AND BIRDS?
EVERYTHING YOU CAN THINK OF! THE WINGLANDS PUTS WINGS ON ANYTHING THAT MAKES IT, WHICH IS A LONG AND STRANGE LIST!
WE EVEN HAVE OUR OWN DEBRIS FIELD OF ALL THE JUNK NOBODY WANTS!
AND WE HAVE AN ENTIRE FLOATING ISLAND... THE MOUSEION!
THAT'S WHERE THE CHUTE SHOP IS!
IS THAT A PLACE FULL OF MOUSES?
NO, IT'S FULL OF BOOKS!
AHHH... THERE IT IS!

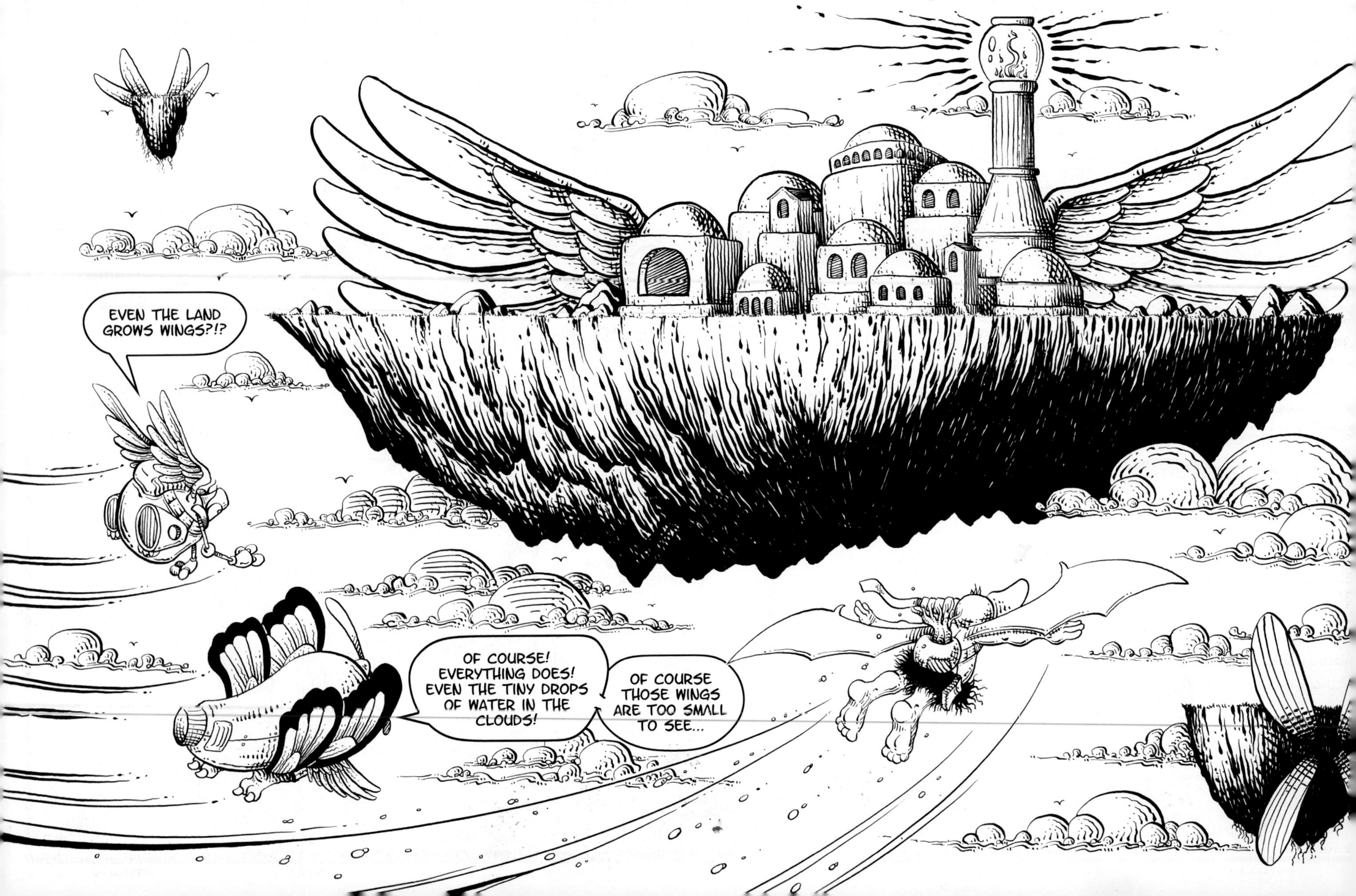
EVEN THE LAND GROWS WINGS?!?
OF COURSE! EVERYTHING DOES! EVEN THE TINY DROPS OF WATER IN THE CLOUDS!
OF COURSE THOSE WINGS ARE TOO SMALL TO SEE...

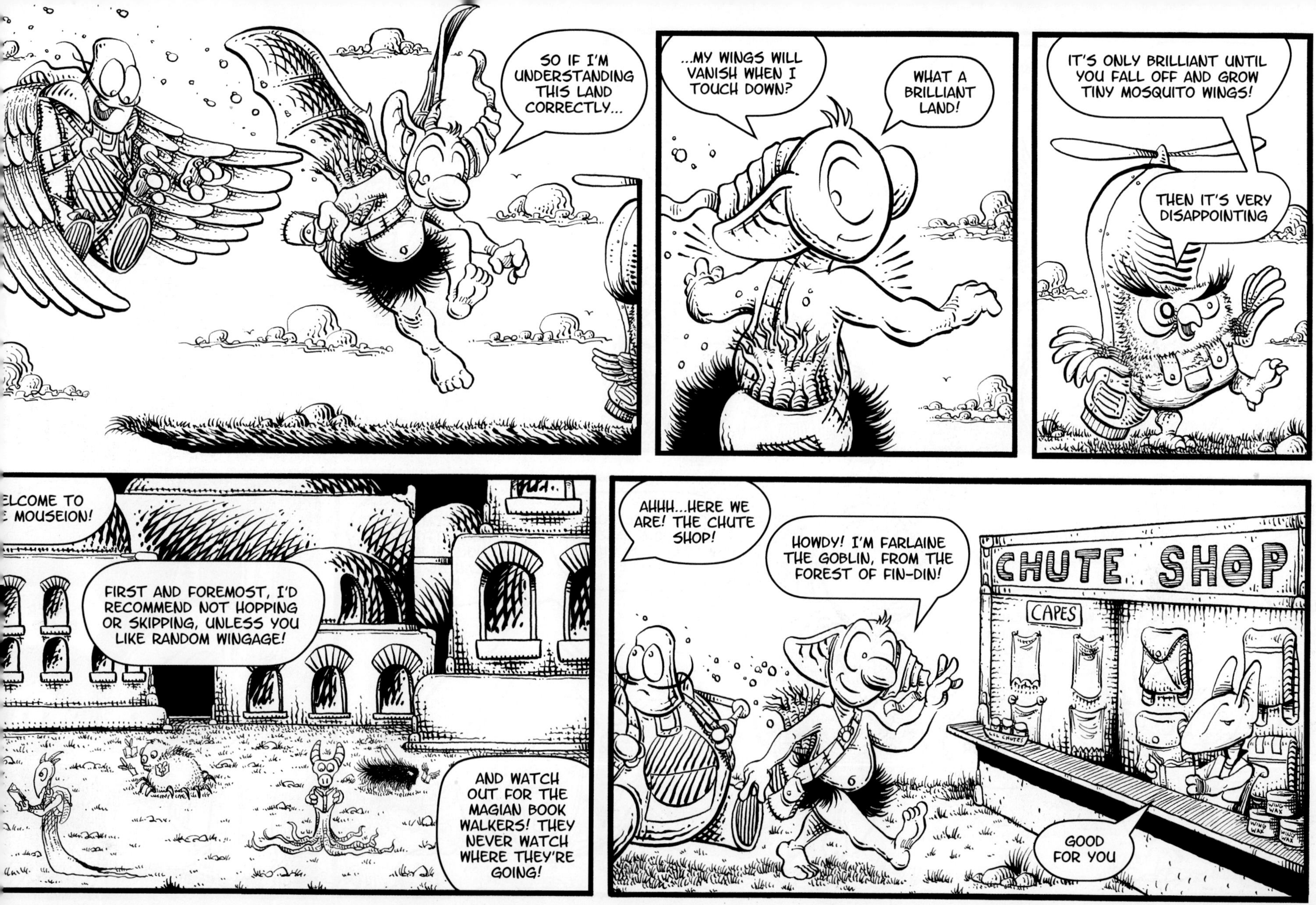
SO IF I'M UNDERSTANDING THIS LAND CORRECTLY...
...MY WINGS WILL VANISH WHEN I TOUCH DOWN?
WHAT A BRILLIANT LAND!
IT'S ONLY BRILLIANT UNTIL YOU FALL OFF AND GROW TINY MOSQUITO WINGS!
THEN IT'S VERY DISAPPOINTING
ELCOME TO
E MOUSEION!
FIRST AND FOREMOST, I'D RECOMMEND NOT HOPPING OR SKIPPING, UNLESS YOU LIKE RANDOM WINGAGE!
AND WATCH OUT FOR THE MAGIAN BOOK WALKERS! THEY NEVER WATCH WHERE THEY'RE GOING!
AHHH...HERE WE ARE! THE CHUTE SHOP!
CHUTE SHOP
CAPES
HOWDY! I'M FARLAINE THE GOBLIN, FROM THE FOREST OF FIN-DIN!
GOOD FOR YOU
WING WAX

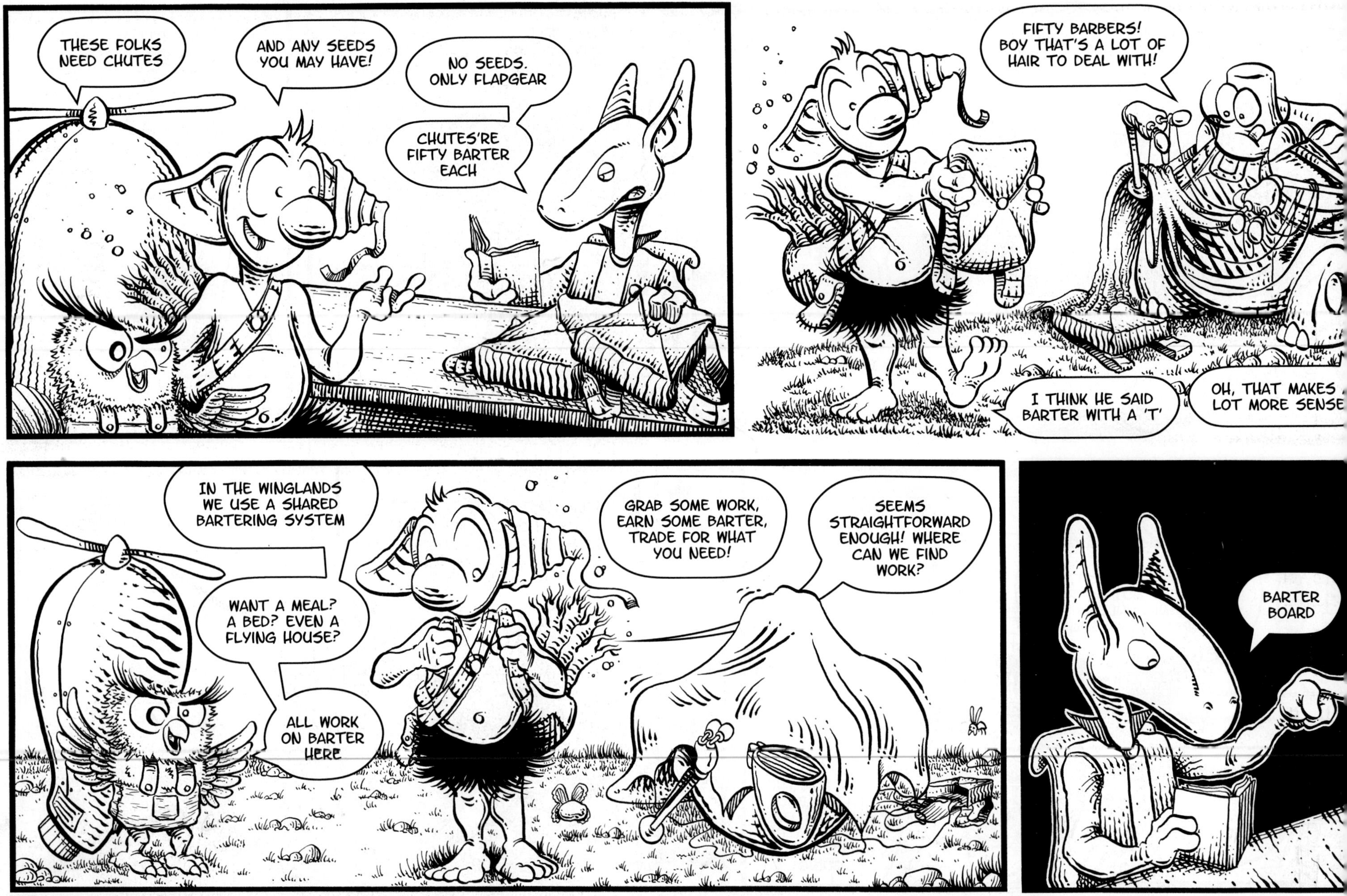
THESE FOLKS NEED CHUTES
AND ANY SEEDS YOU MAY HAVE!
NO SEEDS. ONLY FLAPGEAR
CHUTES'RE FIFTY BARTER EACH
FIFTY BARBERS! BOY THAT'S A LOT OF HAIR TO DEAL WITH!
I THINK HE SAID BARTER WITH A 'T'
OH, THAT MAKES LOT MORE SENSE
IN THE WINGLANDS WE USE A SHARED BARTERING SYSTEM
WANT A MEAL? A BED? EVEN A FLYING HOUSE?
ALL WORK ON BARTER HERE
GRAB SOME WORK, EARN SOME BARTER, TRADE FOR WHAT YOU NEED!
SEEMS STRAIGHTFORWARD ENOUGH! WHERE CAN WE FIND WORK?
BARTER BOARD

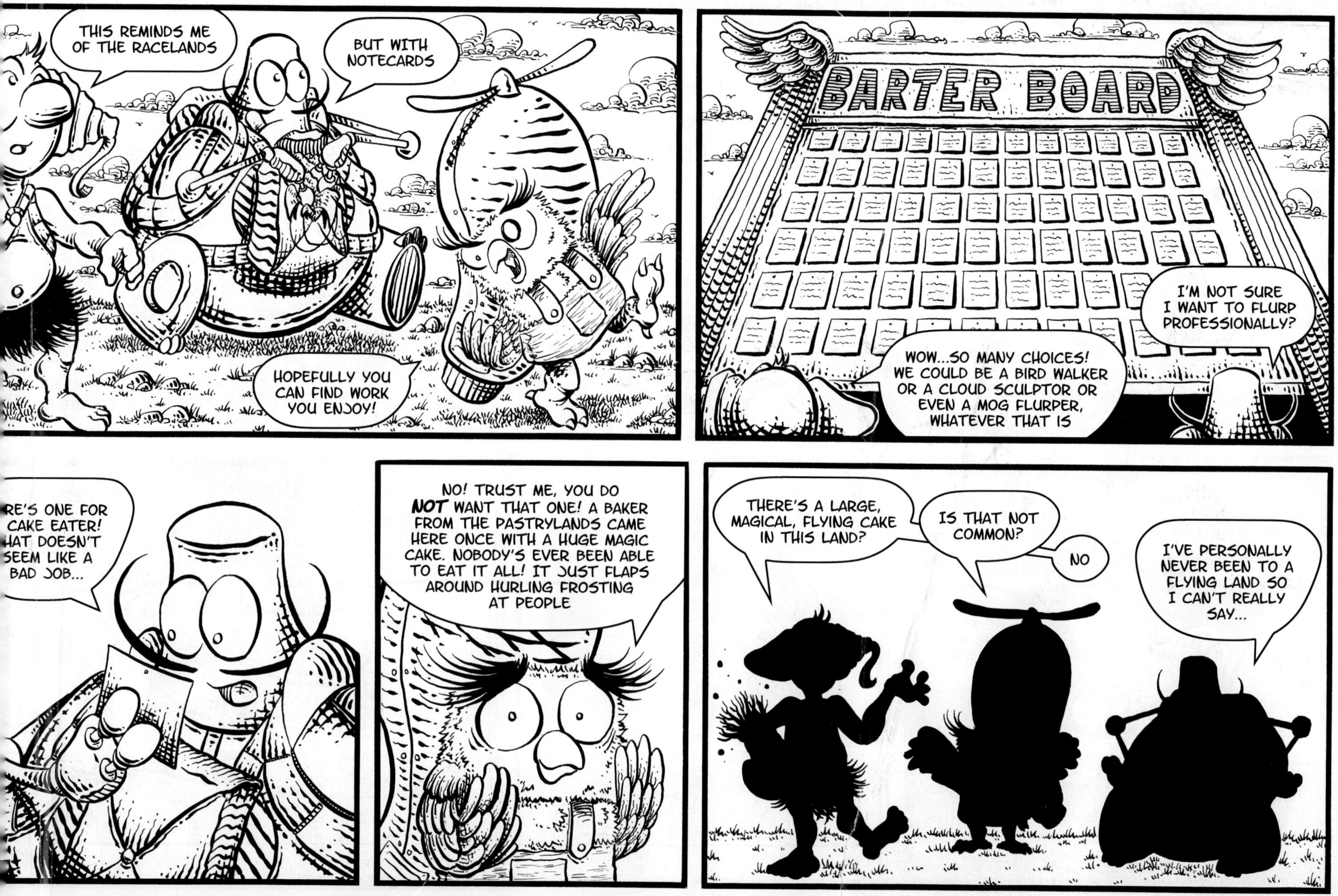
THIS REMINDS ME OF THE RACELANDS
BUT WITH NOTECARDS
HOPEFULLY YOU CAN FIND WORK YOU ENJOY!
BARTER BOARD
WOW...SO MANY CHOICES! WE COULD BE A BIRD WALKER OR A CLOUD SCULPTOR OR EVEN A MOG FLURPER, WHATEVER THAT IS
I'M NOT SURE I WANT TO FLURP PROFESSIONALLY?
RE'S ONE FOR CAKE EATER! HAT DOESN'T SEEM LIKE A BAD JOB...
NO! TRUST ME, YOU DO NOT WANT THAT ONE! A BAKER FROM THE PASTRYLANDS CAME HERE ONCE WITH A HUGE MAGIC CAKE. NOBODY'S EVER BEEN ABLE TO EAT IT ALL! IT JUST FLAPS AROUND HURLING FROSTING AT PEOPLE
THERE'S A LARGE, MAGICAL, FLYING CAKE IN THIS LAND?
IS THAT NOT COMMON?
NO
I'VE PERSONALLY NEVER BEEN TO A FLYING LAND SO I CAN'T REALLY SAY...

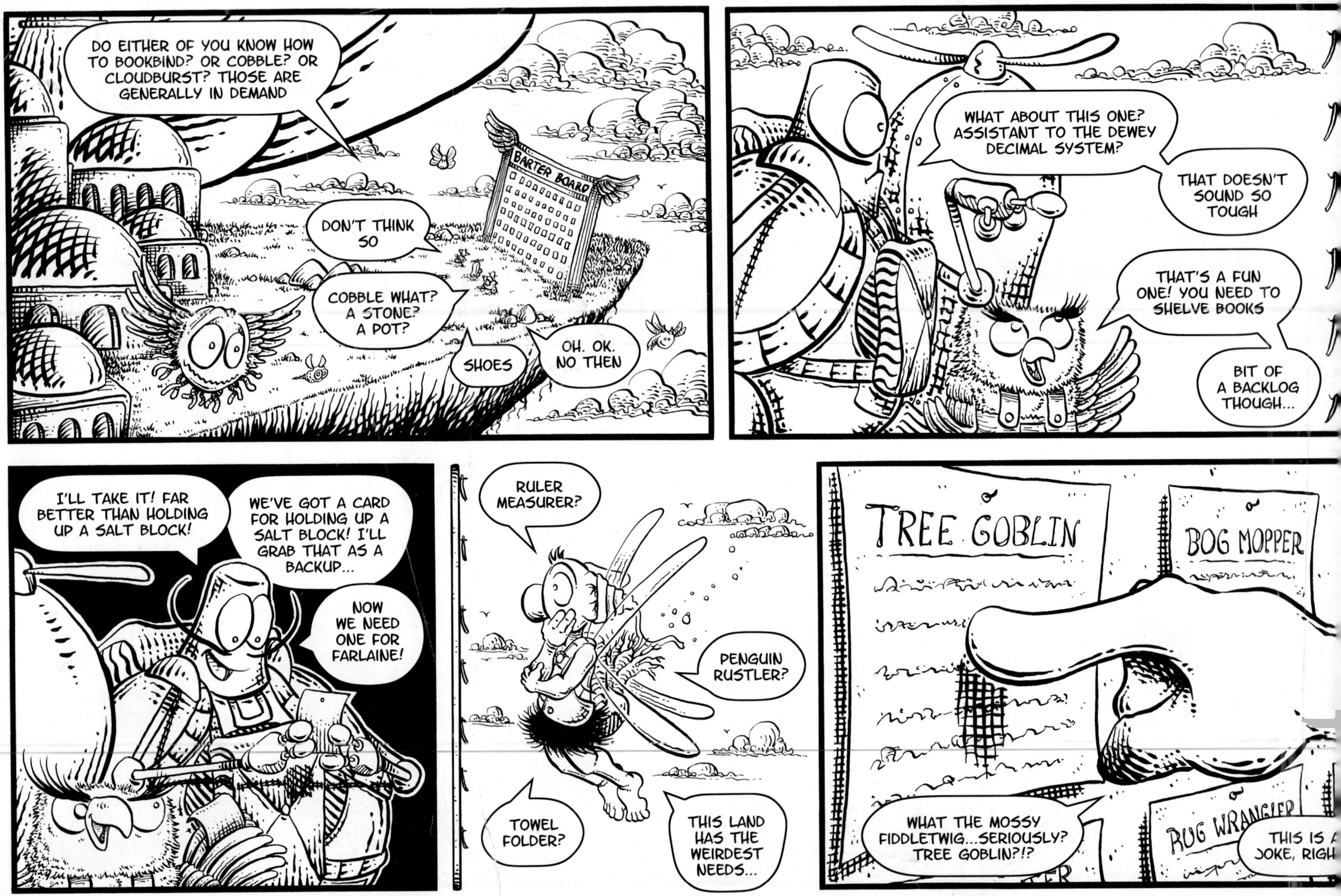
DO EITHER OF YOU KNOW HOW TO BOOKBIND? OR COBBLE? OR CLOUDBURST? THOSE ARE GENERALLY IN DEMAND
BARTER BOARD
DON'T THINK SO
COBBLE WHAT? A STONE? A POT?
SHOES
OH. OK. NO THEN
WHAT ABOUT THIS ONE? ASSISTANT TO THE DEWEY DECIMAL SYSTEM?
THAT DOESN'T SOUND SO TOUGH
THAT'S A FUN ONE! YOU NEED TO SHELVE BOOKS
BIT OF A BACKLOG THOUGH...
I'LL TAKE IT! FAR BETTER THAN HOLDING UP A SALT BLOCK!
WE'VE GOT A CARD FOR HOLDING UP A SALT BLOCK! I'LL GRAB THAT AS A BACKUP...
NOW WE NEED ONE FOR FARLAINE!
RULER MEASURER?
PENGUIN RUSTLER?
TOWEL FOLDER?
THIS LAND HAS THE WEIRDEST NEEDS...
TREE GOBLIN
BOG MOPPER
RUG WRANGLER
WHAT THE MOSSY FIDDLETWIG...SERIOUSLY? TREE GOBLIN?!?
THIS IS A JOKE, RIGH

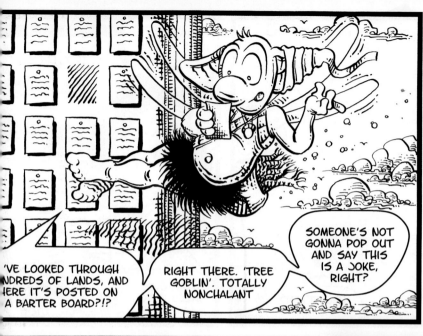

I'VE LOOKED THROUGH HUNDREDS OF LANDS, AND HERE IT'S POSTED ON A BARTER BOARD?!?

RIGHT THERE. 'TREE GOBLIN'. TOTALLY NONCHALANT

SOMEONE'S NOT GONNA POP OUT AND SAY THIS IS A JOKE, RIGHT?

THAT JOB'S BEEN POSTED FOR GENERATIONS! NEVER GETS PICKED BECAUSE TREE GOBLINS NEVER VISIT!

BUT...WE'RE IN THE SKY? HOW CAN THERE BE A FOREST UP HERE??

...OTS. LOTS AND LOTS OF POTS

A POTTED FOREST! I'VE NEVER HEARD OF SUCH A THING!

SO EACH PLANT IS ON ITS OWN? NO ROOTS TOUCH?

GENERALLY, EXCEPT FOR THE KUDZU. KUDZU CAN'T BE CONTAINED!!

ARE THERE ANY STRANGE RULES?

ANY FINE PRINT THAT YOU'RE GONNA TAKE IT AWAY NEXT WEEK OR MAKE ME RACE FOR IT OR ANYTHING?

MAKE YOU RACE FOR IT? NO, NO, YOU'RE WELCOME TO THE JOB AS LONG AS YOU WANT IT! WE'D BE THRILLED TO HAVE A TREE GOBLIN UP HERE! WE'RE ALL BORED OF EATING ONLY PASTA AND POTATOES...

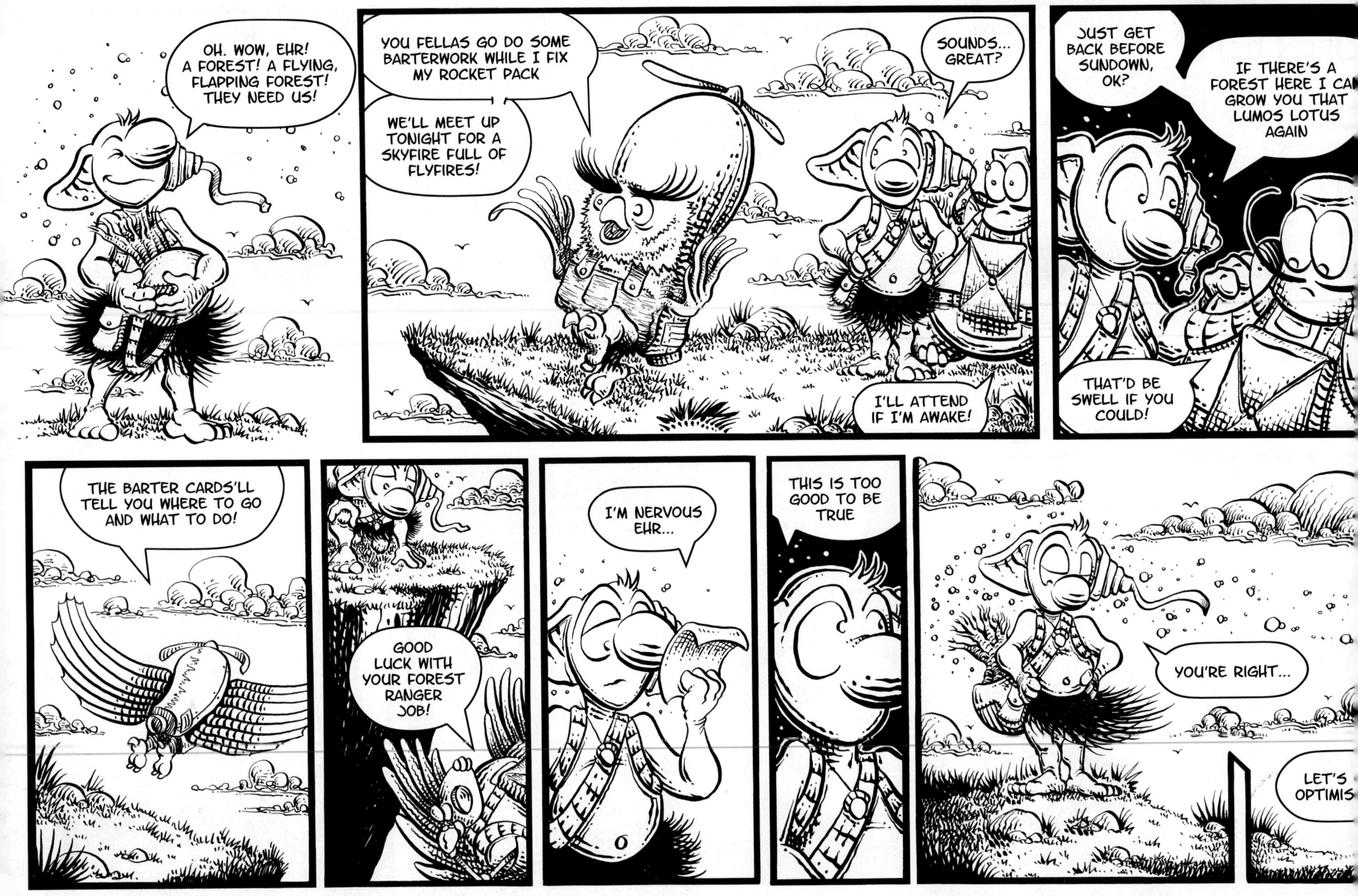
OH. WOW, EHR! A FOREST! A FLYING, FLAPPING FOREST! THEY NEED US!
YOU FELLAS GO DO SOME BARTERWORK WHILE I FIX MY ROCKET PACK
WE'LL MEET UP TONIGHT FOR A SKYFIRE FULL OF FLYFIRES!
SOUNDS... GREAT?
I'LL ATTEND IF I'M AWAKE!
JUST GET BACK BEFORE SUNDOWN, OK?
IF THERE'S A FOREST HERE I CA GROW YOU THAT LUMOS LOTUS AGAIN
THAT'D BE SWELL IF YOU COULD!
THE BARTER CARDS'LL TELL YOU WHERE TO GO AND WHAT TO DO!
GOOD LUCK WITH YOUR FOREST RANGER JOB!
I'M NERVOUS EHR...
THIS IS TOO GOOD TO BE TRUE
YOU'RE RIGHT...
LET'S OPTIMIS

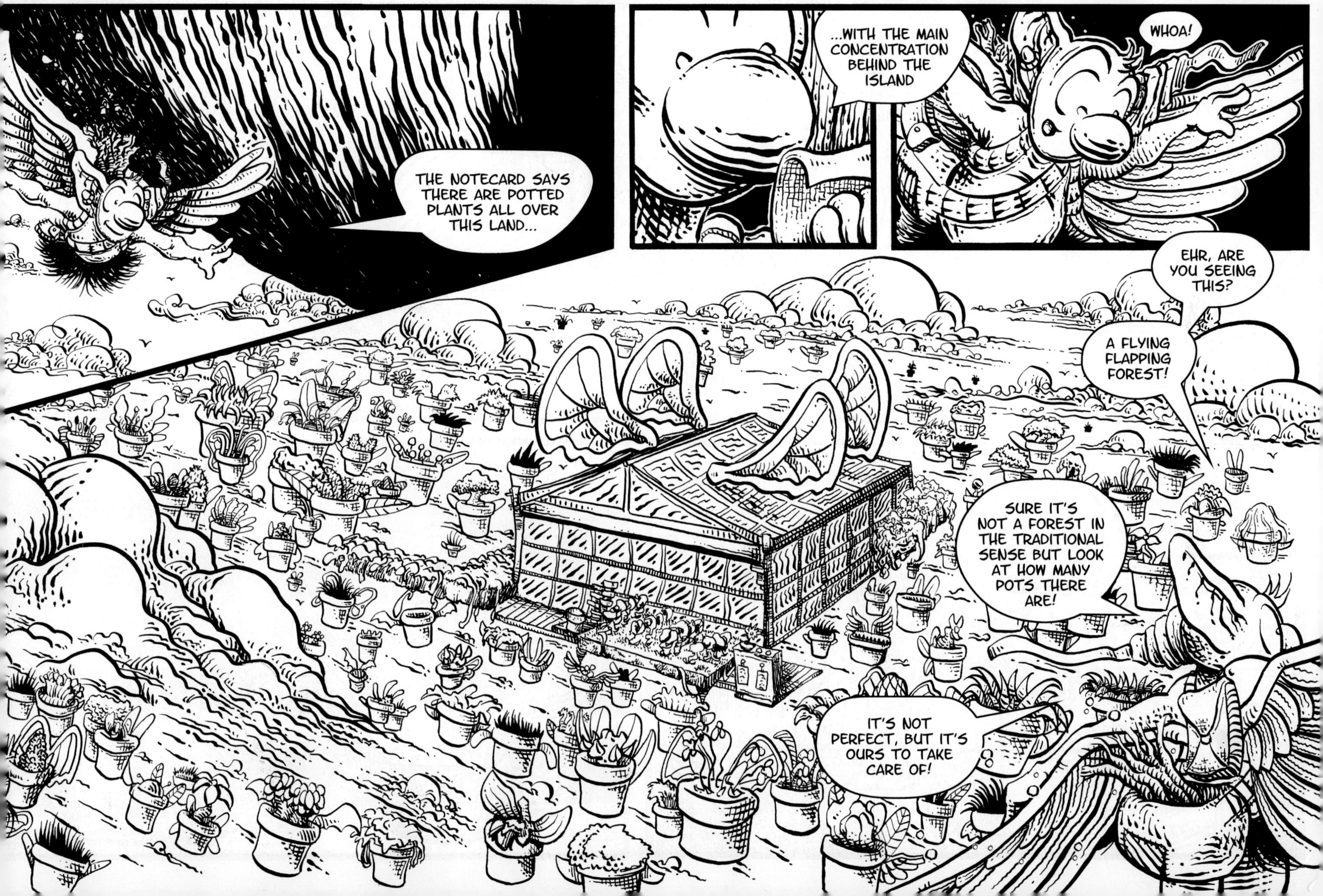
THE NOTECARD SAYS THERE ARE POTTED PLANTS ALL OVER THIS LAND...
...WITH THE MAIN CONCENTRATION BEHIND THE ISLAND
WHOA!
EHR, ARE YOU SEEING THIS?
A FLYING FLAPPING FOREST!
SURE IT'S NOT A FOREST IN THE TRADITIONAL SENSE BUT LOOK AT HOW MANY POTS THERE ARE!
IT'S NOT PERFECT, BUT IT'S OURS TO TAKE CARE OF!

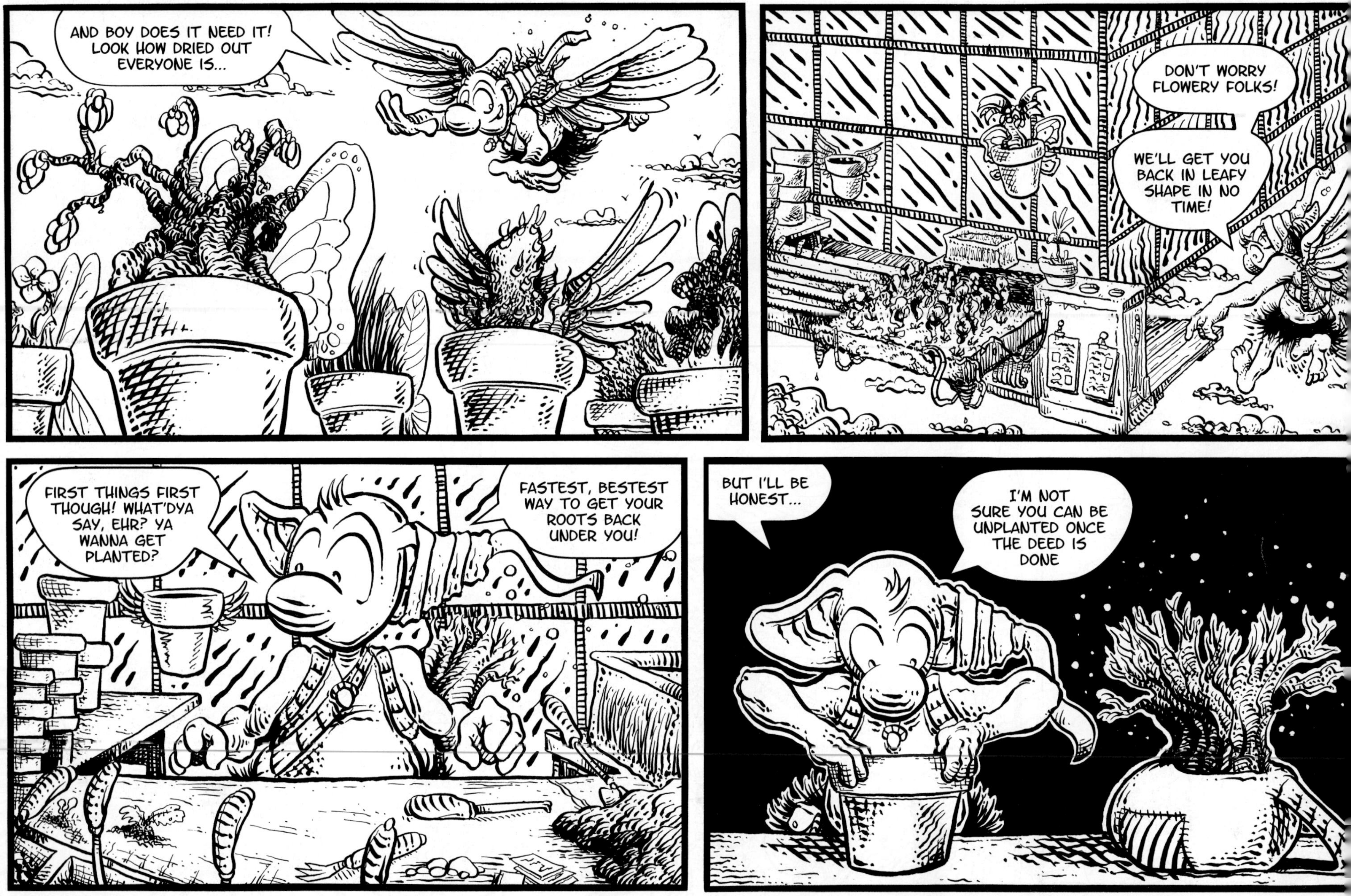
AND BOY DOES IT NEED IT! LOOK HOW DRIED OUT EVERYONE IS...
DON'T WORRY FLOWERY FOLKS!
WE'LL GET YOU BACK IN LEAFY SHAPE IN NO TIME!
FIRST THINGS FIRST THOUGH! WHAT'DYA SAY, EHR? YA WANNA GET PLANTED?
FASTEST, BESTEST WAY TO GET YOUR ROOTS BACK UNDER YOU!
BUT I'LL BE HONEST...
I'M NOT SURE YOU CAN BE UNPLANTED ONCE THE DEED IS DONE

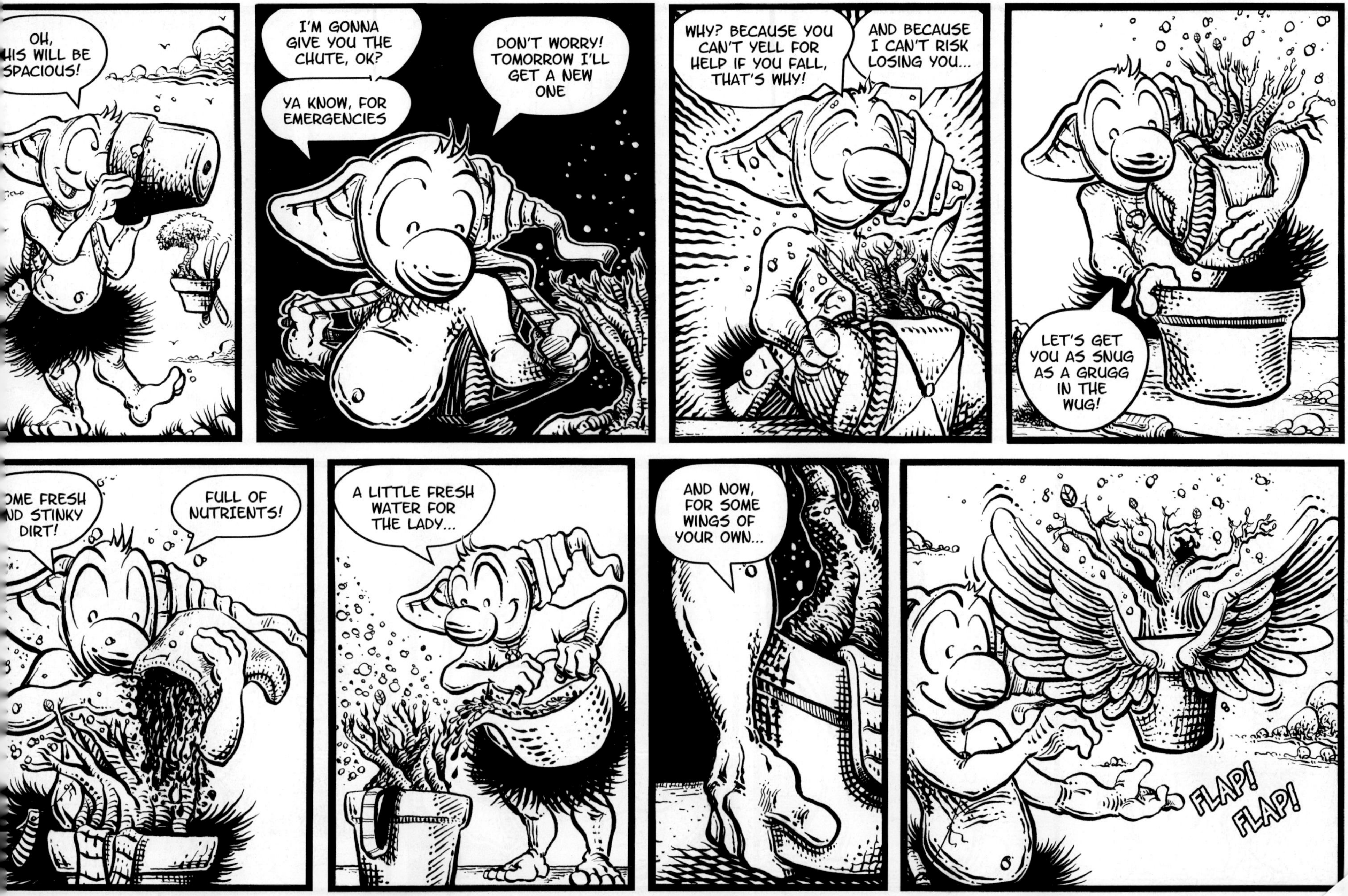
OH, HIS WILL BE SPACIOUS!
I'M GONNA GIVE YOU THE CHUTE, OK?
YA KNOW, FOR EMERGENCIES
DON'T WORRY! TOMORROW I'LL GET A NEW ONE
WHY? BECAUSE YOU CAN'T YELL FOR HELP IF YOU FALL, THAT'S WHY!
AND BECAUSE I CAN'T RISK LOSING YOU...
LET'S GET YOU AS SNUG AS A GRUGG IN THE WUG!
OME FRESH ND STINKY DIRT!
FULL OF NUTRIENTS!
A LITTLE FRESH WATER FOR THE LADY...
AND NOW, FOR SOME WINGS OF YOUR OWN...
FLAP! FLAP!

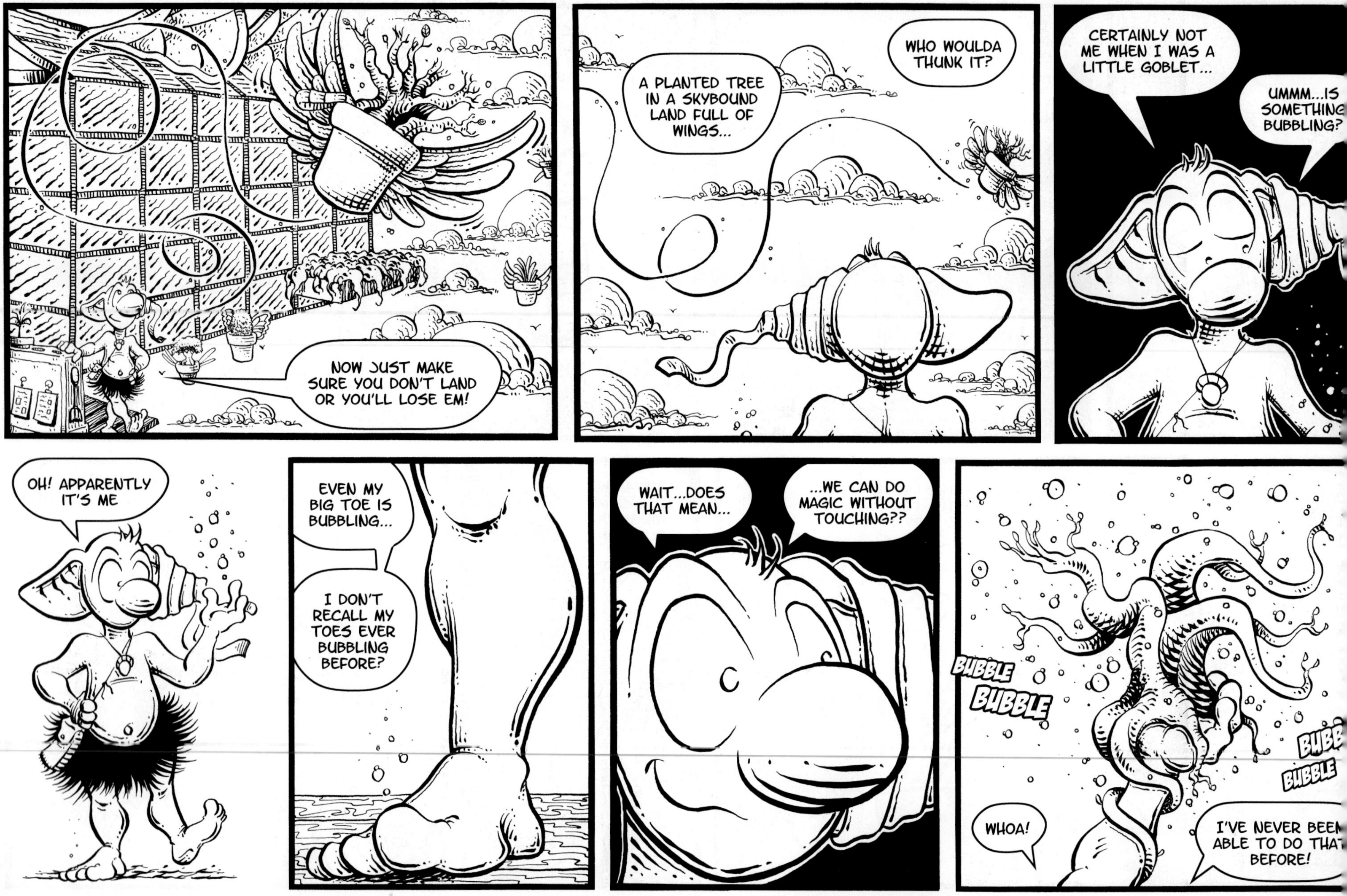
NOW JUST MAKE SURE YOU DON'T LAND OR YOU'LL LOSE EM!
A PLANTED TREE IN A SKYBOUND LAND FULL OF WINGS...
WHO WOULDA THUNK IT?
CERTAINLY NOT ME WHEN I WAS A LITTLE GOBLET...
UMMM...IS SOMETHING BUBBLING?
OH! APPARENTLY IT'S ME
EVEN MY BIG TOE IS BUBBLING...
I DON'T RECALL MY TOES EVER BUBBLING BEFORE?
WAIT...DOES THAT MEAN...
...WE CAN DO MAGIC WITHOUT TOUCHING??
BUBBLE
BUBBLE
BUBBLE
WHOA!
I'VE NEVER BEEN ABLE TO DO THAT BEFORE!

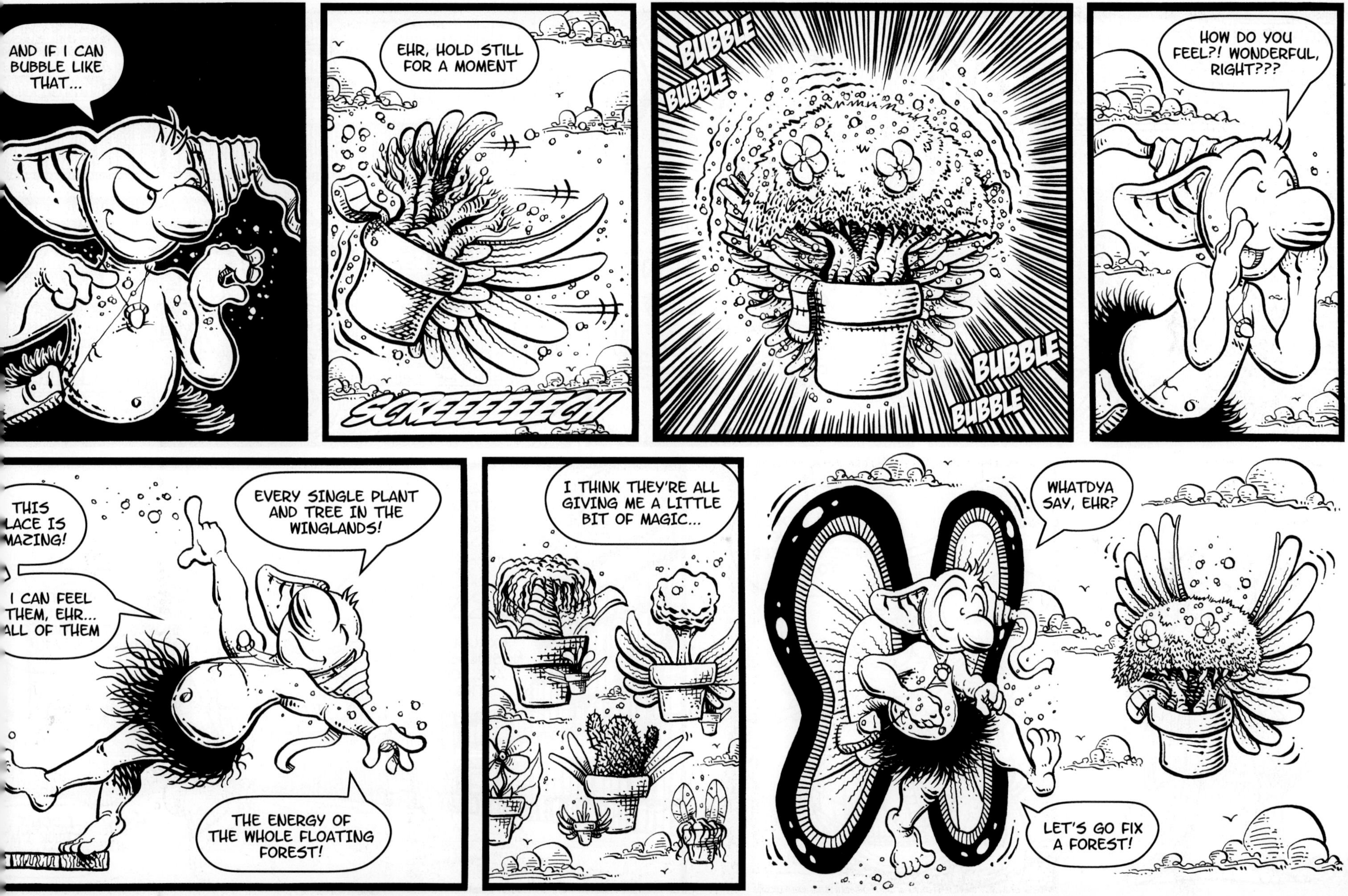
AND IF I CAN BUBBLE LIKE THAT...
EHR, HOLD STILL FOR A MOMENT
SCREEEEEEEECH
BUBBLE BUBBLE
BUBBLE BUBBLE
HOW DO YOU FEEL?! WONDERFUL, RIGHT???
THIS LACE IS MAZING!
I CAN FEEL THEM, EHR... ALL OF THEM
EVERY SINGLE PLANT AND TREE IN THE WINGLANDS!
THE ENERGY OF THE WHOLE FLOATING FOREST!
I THINK THEY'RE ALL GIVING ME A LITTLE BIT OF MAGIC...
WHATDYA SAY, EHR?
LET'S GO FIX A FOREST!

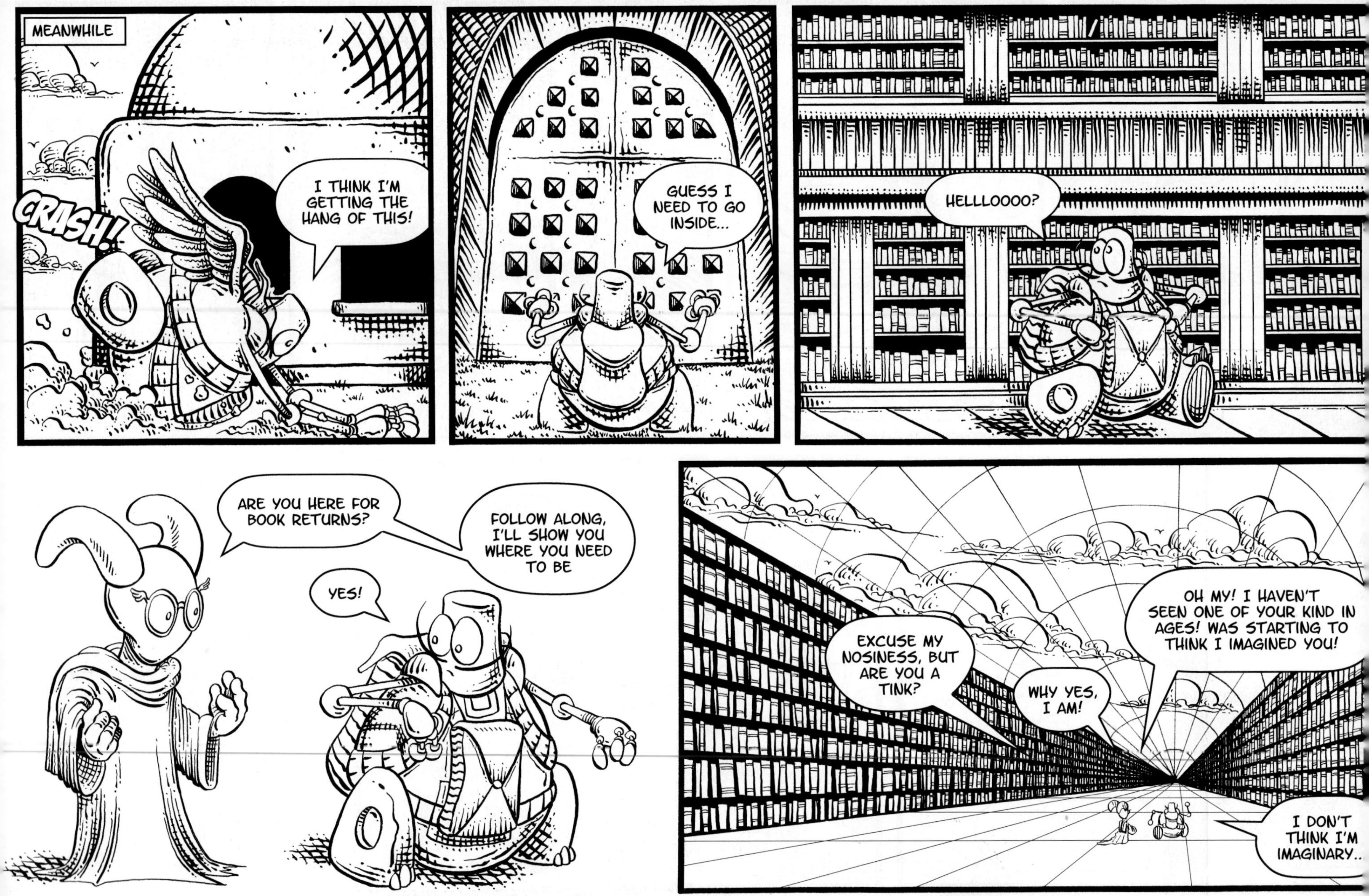
MEANWHILE
CRASH!
I THINK I'M GETTING THE HANG OF THIS!
GUESS I NEED TO GO INSIDE...
HELLLOOOO?
ARE YOU HERE FOR BOOK RETURNS?
YES!
FOLLOW ALONG, I'LL SHOW YOU WHERE YOU NEED TO BE
EXCUSE MY NOSINESS, BUT ARE YOU A TINK?
WHY YES, I AM!
OH MY! I HAVEN'T SEEN ONE OF YOUR KIND IN AGES! WAS STARTING TO THINK I IMAGINED YOU!
I DON'T THINK I'M IMAGINARY...

NOW I SENSE SOMETHING IS A BIT FFERENT ABOUT YOU. U SEEM MORE MAGICAL THAN I REMEMBER TINKS BEING?
I'M MAGICAL?
OF COURSE YOU ARE! HOW ELSE CAN YOU DO THE THINGS YOU CAN DO?
SCIENTIFIC ENGINEERING?
WELL, SURE, MOSTLY, BUT IT ALSO NEEDS A DAB OF MAGIC TO MAKE IT SPARK!
ALL TINKS ARE POWERED BY A LITTLE MAGIC, BUT YOU SIR, ARE POWERED BY A LOT!
I WAS NOT AWARE OF THAT
HERE WE ARE! HE RETURN PILE!
WOW, THAT'S ONE BIG PILE OF BOOKS
WE'RE VORACIOUS READERS HERE
THIS IS GONNA BE SO FUN!

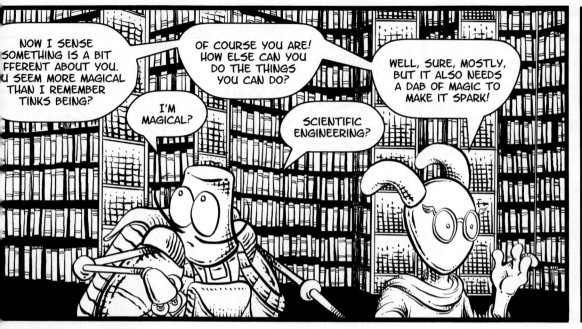

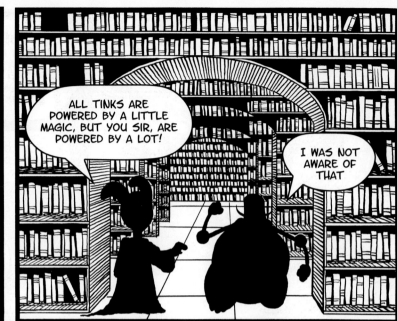

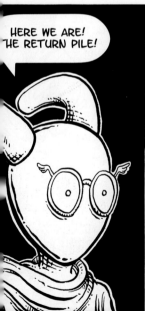

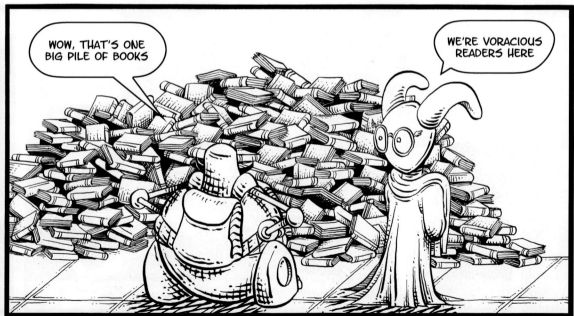

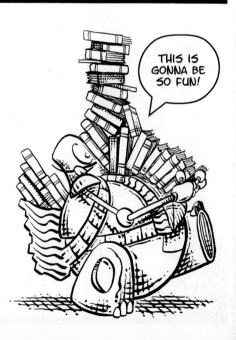

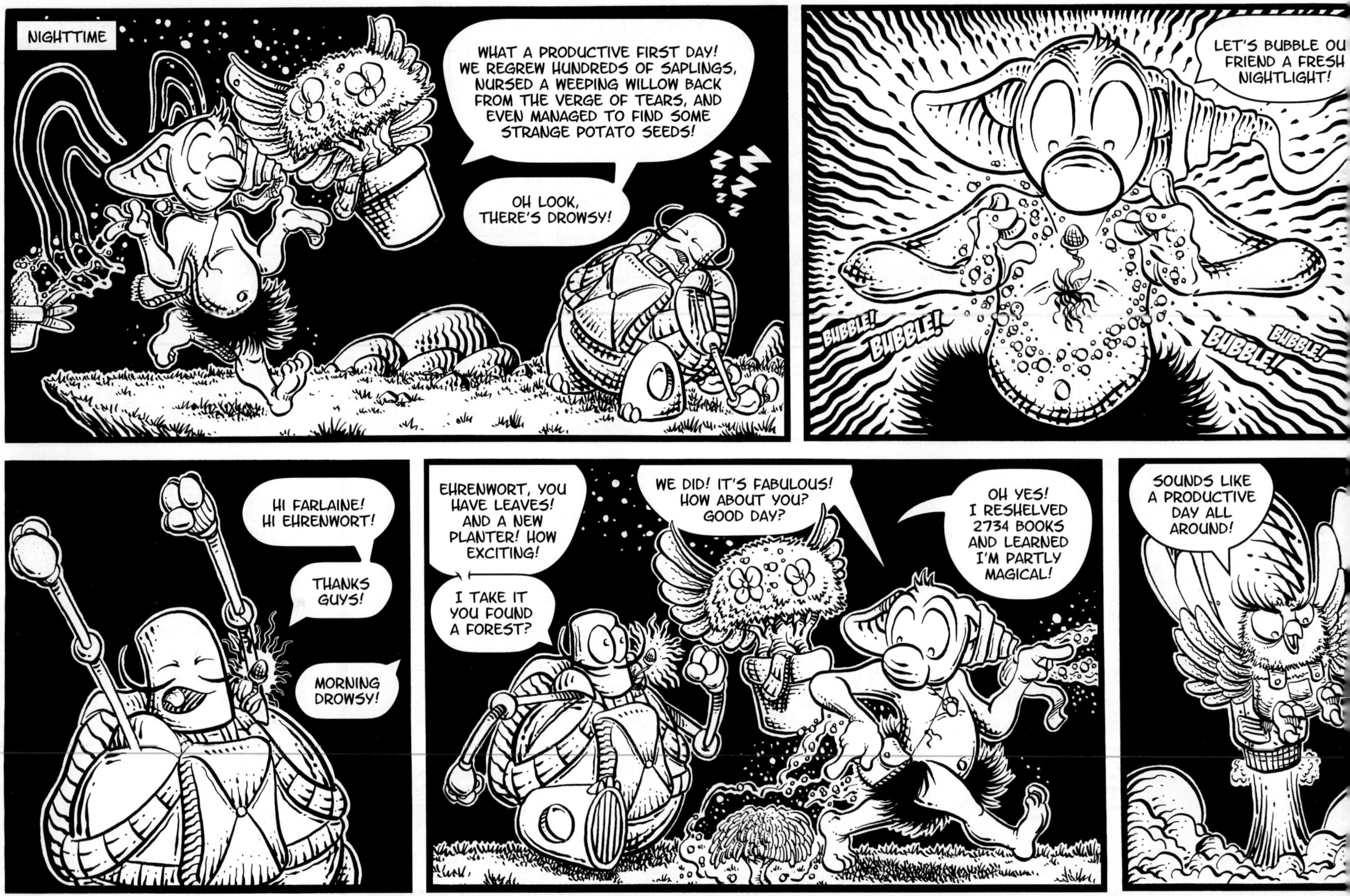
NIGHTTIME
WHAT A PRODUCTIVE FIRST DAY! WE REGREW HUNDREDS OF SAPLINGS, NURSED A WEEPING WILLOW BACK FROM THE VERGE OF TEARS, AND EVEN MANAGED TO FIND SOME STRANGE POTATO SEEDS!
OH LOOK, THERE'S DROWSY!
LET'S BUBBLE OU FRIEND A FRESH NIGHTLIGHT!
BUBBLE! BUBBLE!
BUBBLE! BUBBLE!
HI FARLAINE! HI EHRENWORT!
THANKS GUYS!
MORNING DROWSY!
EHRENWORT, YOU HAVE LEAVES! AND A NEW PLANTER! HOW EXCITING!
I TAKE IT YOU FOUND A FOREST?
WE DID! IT'S FABULOUS! HOW ABOUT YOU? GOOD DAY?
OH YES! I RESHELVED 2734 BOOKS AND LEARNED I'M PARTLY MAGICAL!
SOUNDS LIKE A PRODUCTIVE DAY ALL AROUND!

IS WAY TO
E SKYFIRE!
WHAT'S A
SKYFIRE?
SEE UP
AHEAD?
OOOOHHHH...
IN THE
WINGLANDS EVEN
FIRE GROWS
WINGS!
THAT'S
BEAUTIFUL!
HELLO
ALL
HI!
HOWDY
HEY
HEYO
EVENING! DON'T RECALL
MEETING YOU BEFORE?
WE JUST ARRIVED! I'M FARLAINE.
THE SHRUB'S EHRENWORT.
THE TINK'S DROWSY.
I'M GERFUDDLE!
WELCOME!
HOW'D YOU FOLKS
MANAGE TO GET
UP HERE?
FARLAINE MADE LEAF
WINGS AND FLAPPED
US UP. YOU?
LADDER

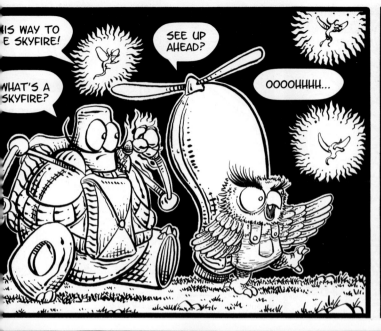

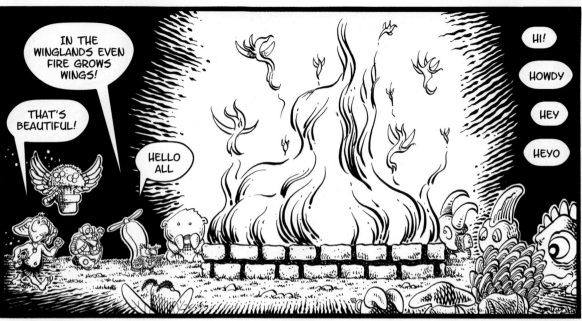

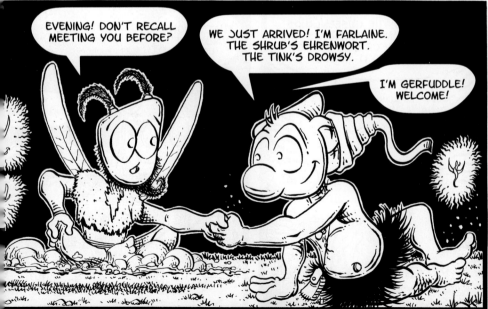

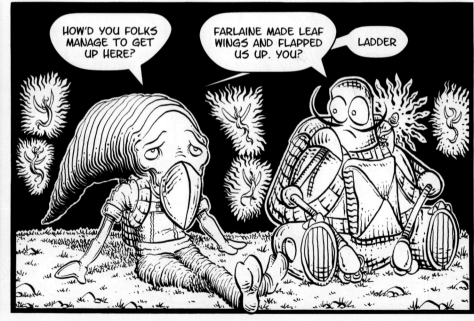

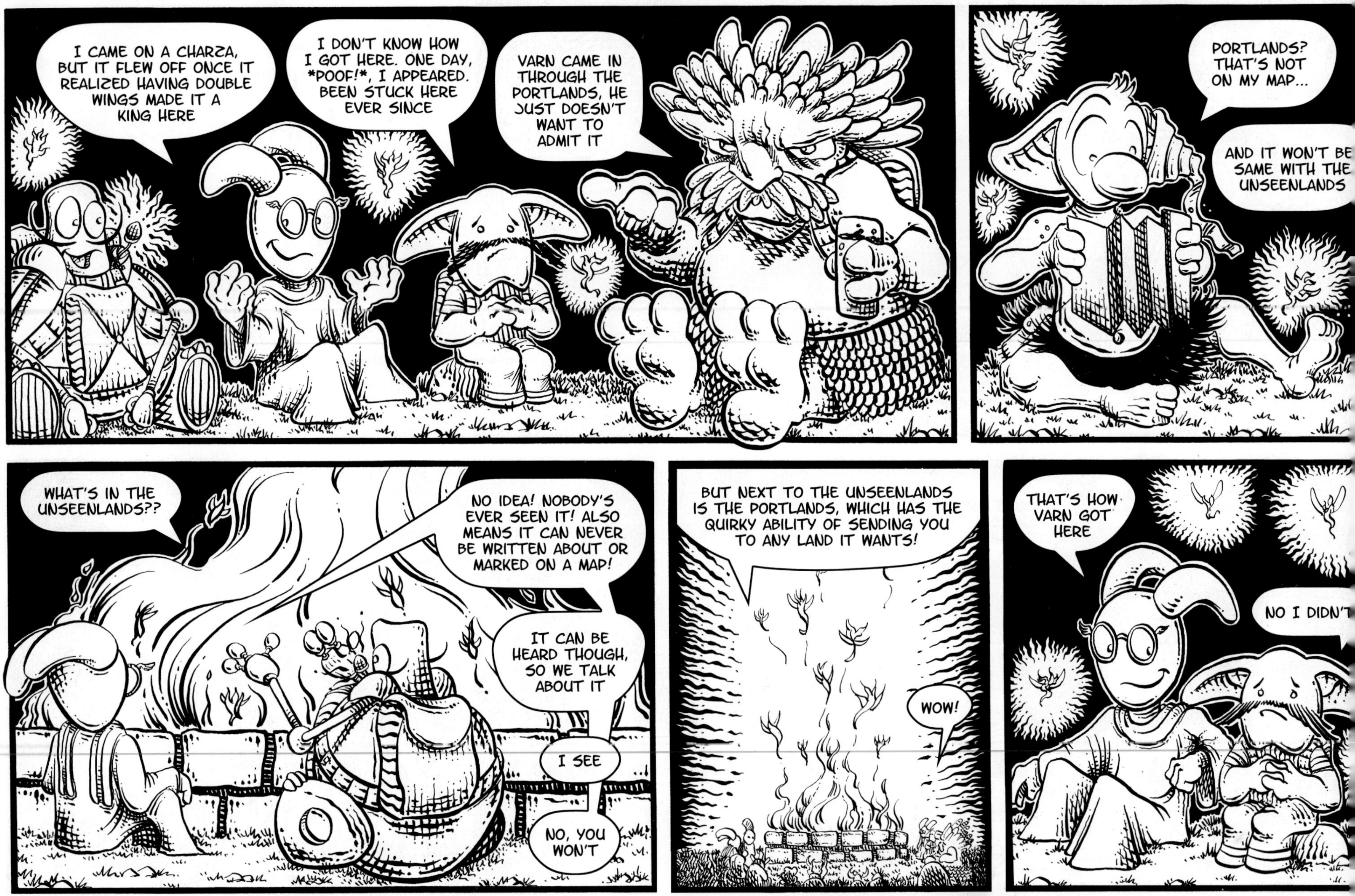

I CAME ON A CHARZA, BUT IT FLEW OFF ONCE IT REALIZED HAVING DOUBLE WINGS MADE IT A KING HERE
I DON'T KNOW HOW I GOT HERE. ONE DAY, *POOF!*, I APPEARED. BEEN STUCK HERE EVER SINCE
VARN CAME IN THROUGH THE PORTLANDS, HE JUST DOESN'T WANT TO ADMIT IT
PORTLANDS? THAT'S NOT ON MY MAP...
AND IT WON'T BE SAME WITH THE UNSEENLANDS
WHAT'S IN THE UNSEENLANDS??
NO IDEA! NOBODY'S EVER SEEN IT! ALSO MEANS IT CAN NEVER BE WRITTEN ABOUT OR MARKED ON A MAP!
IT CAN BE HEARD THOUGH, SO WE TALK ABOUT IT
I SEE
NO, YOU WON'T
BUT NEXT TO THE UNSEENLANDS IS THE PORTLANDS, WHICH HAS THE QUIRKY ABILITY OF SENDING YOU TO ANY LAND IT WANTS!
WOW!
THAT'S HOW VARN GOT HERE
NO I DIDN'T

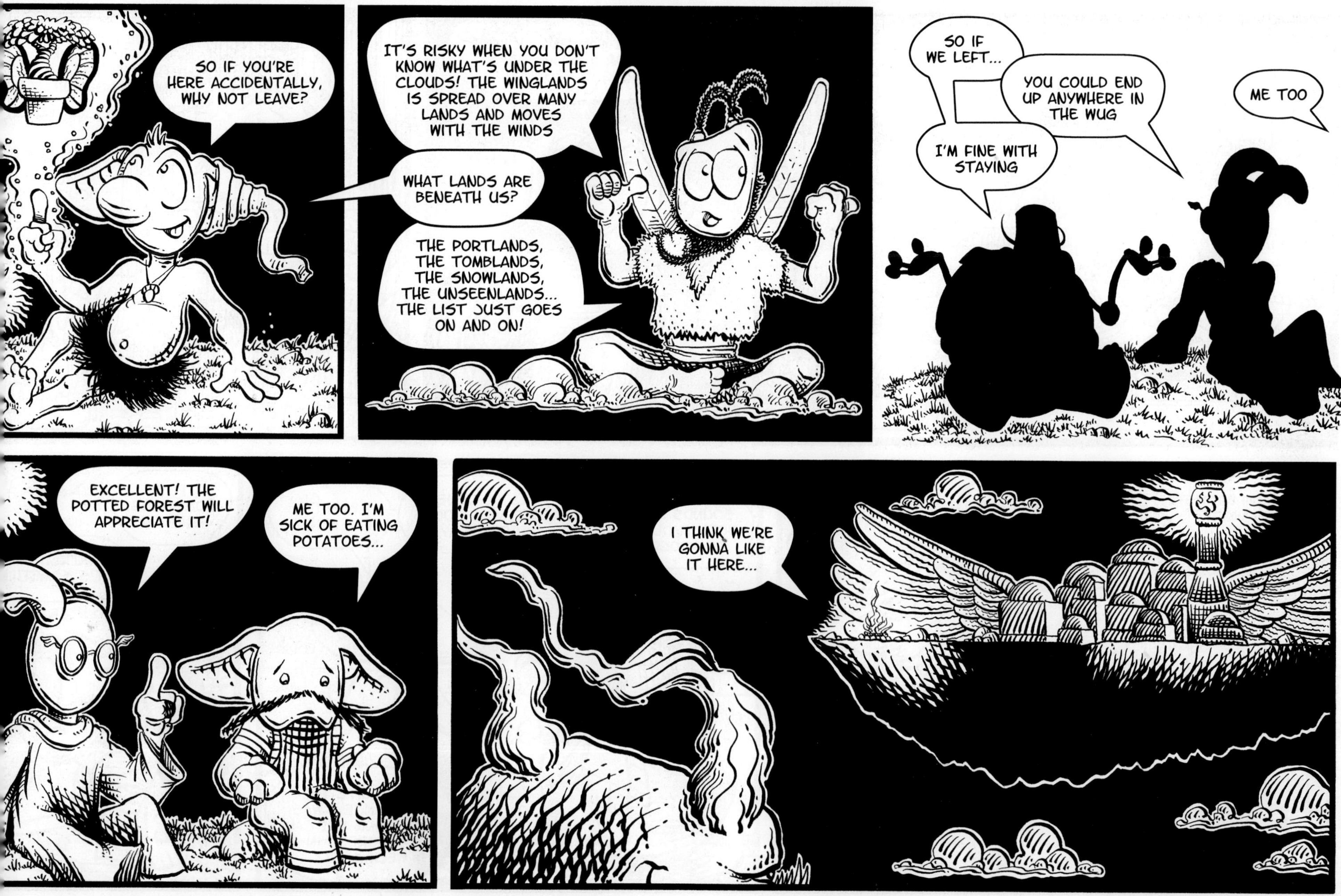
SO IF YOU'RE HERE ACCIDENTALLY, WHY NOT LEAVE?
IT'S RISKY WHEN YOU DON'T KNOW WHAT'S UNDER THE CLOUDS! THE WINGLANDS IS SPREAD OVER MANY LANDS AND MOVES WITH THE WINDS
WHAT LANDS ARE BENEATH US?
THE PORTLANDS, THE TOMBLANDS, THE SNOWLANDS, THE UNSEENLANDS... THE LIST JUST GOES ON AND ON!
SO IF WE LEFT...
YOU COULD END UP ANYWHERE IN THE WUG
I'M FINE WITH STAYING
ME TOO
EXCELLENT! THE POTTED FOREST WILL APPRECIATE IT!
ME TOO. I'M SICK OF EATING POTATOES...
I THINK WE'RE GONNA LIKE IT HERE...

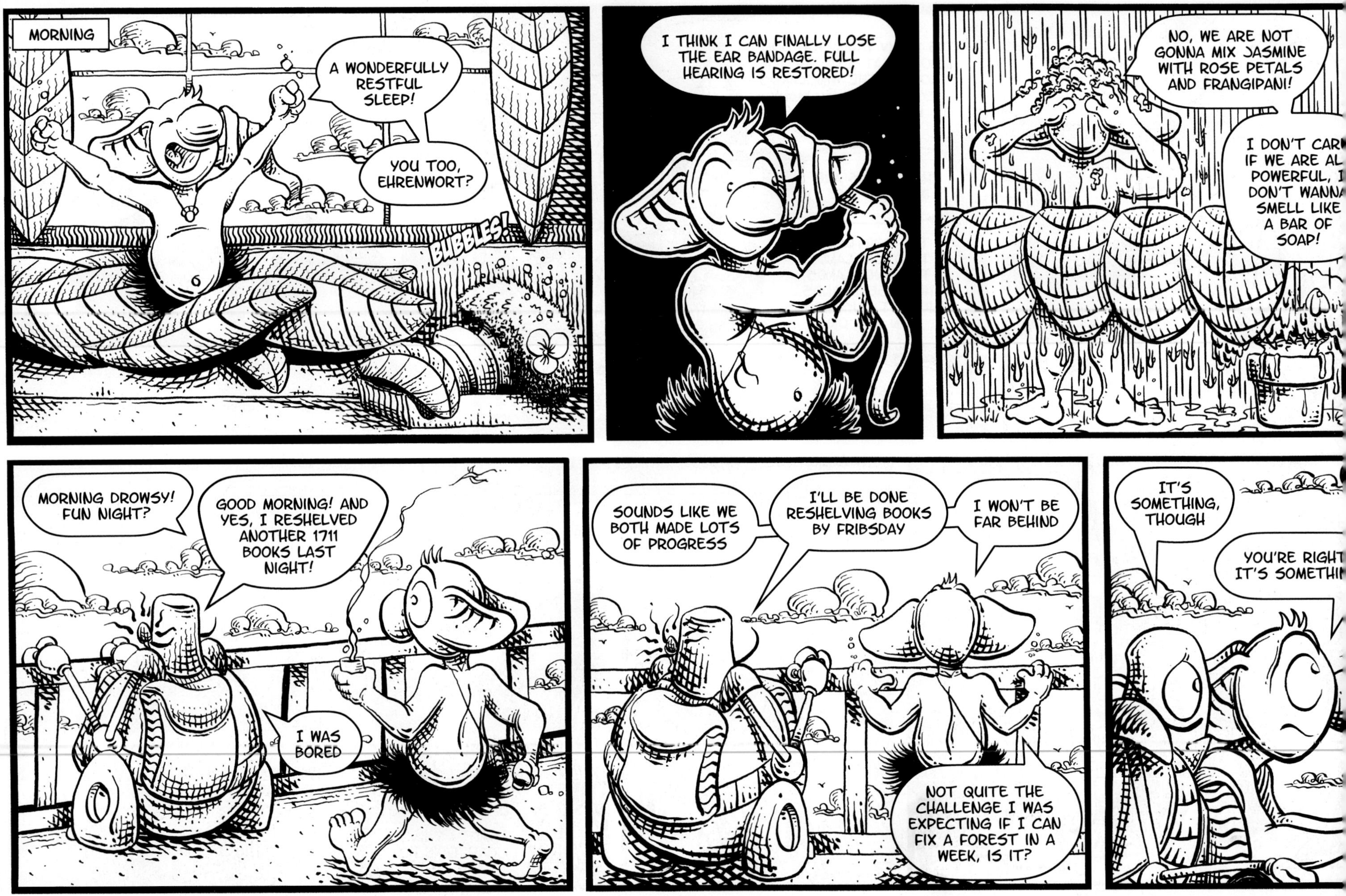
MORNING
A WONDERFULLY RESTFUL SLEEP!
YOU TOO, EHRENWORT?
BUBBLES!
I THINK I CAN FINALLY LOSE THE EAR BANDAGE. FULL HEARING IS RESTORED!
NO, WE ARE NOT GONNA MIX JASMINE WITH ROSE PETALS AND FRANGIPANI!
I DON'T CAR
IF WE ARE AL
POWERFUL, I
DON'T WANNA
SMELL LIKE
A BAR OF
SOAP!
MORNING DROWSY! FUN NIGHT?
GOOD MORNING! AND YES, I RESHELVED ANOTHER 1711 BOOKS LAST NIGHT!
I WAS BORED
SOUNDS LIKE WE BOTH MADE LOTS OF PROGRESS
I'LL BE DONE RESHELVING BOOKS BY FRIBSDAY
I WON'T BE FAR BEHIND
NOT QUITE THE CHALLENGE I WAS EXPECTING IF I CAN FIX A FOREST IN A WEEK, IS IT?
IT'S SOMETHING, THOUGH
YOU'RE RIGHT
IT'S SOMETHI

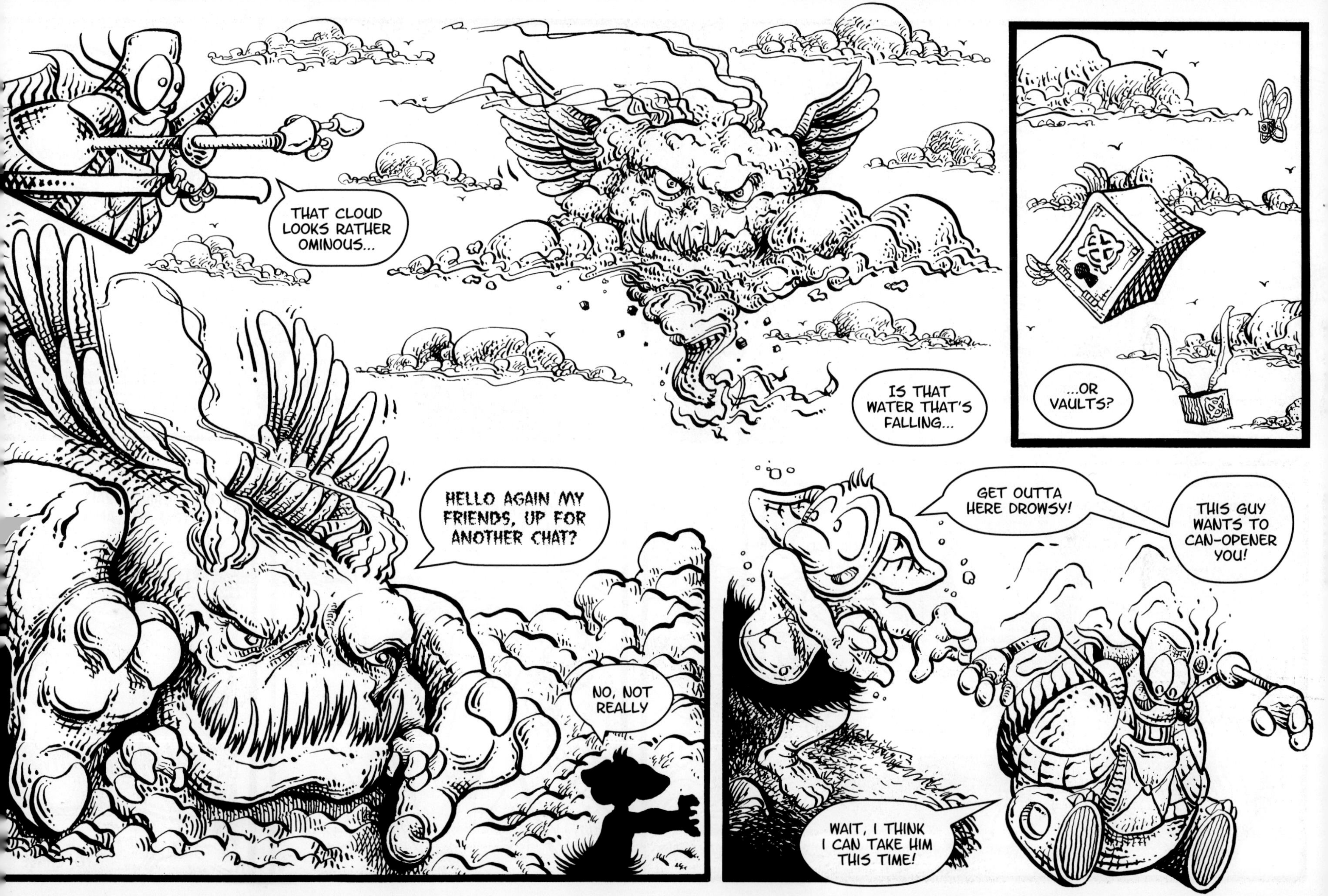
THAT CLOUD LOOKS RATHER OMINOUS...
IS THAT WATER THAT'S FALLING...
...OR VAULTS?
HELLO AGAIN MY FRIENDS, UP FOR ANOTHER CHAT?
NO, NOT REALLY
GET OUTTA HERE DROWSY!
THIS GUY WANTS TO CAN-OPENER YOU!
WAIT, I THINK I CAN TAKE HIM THIS TIME!

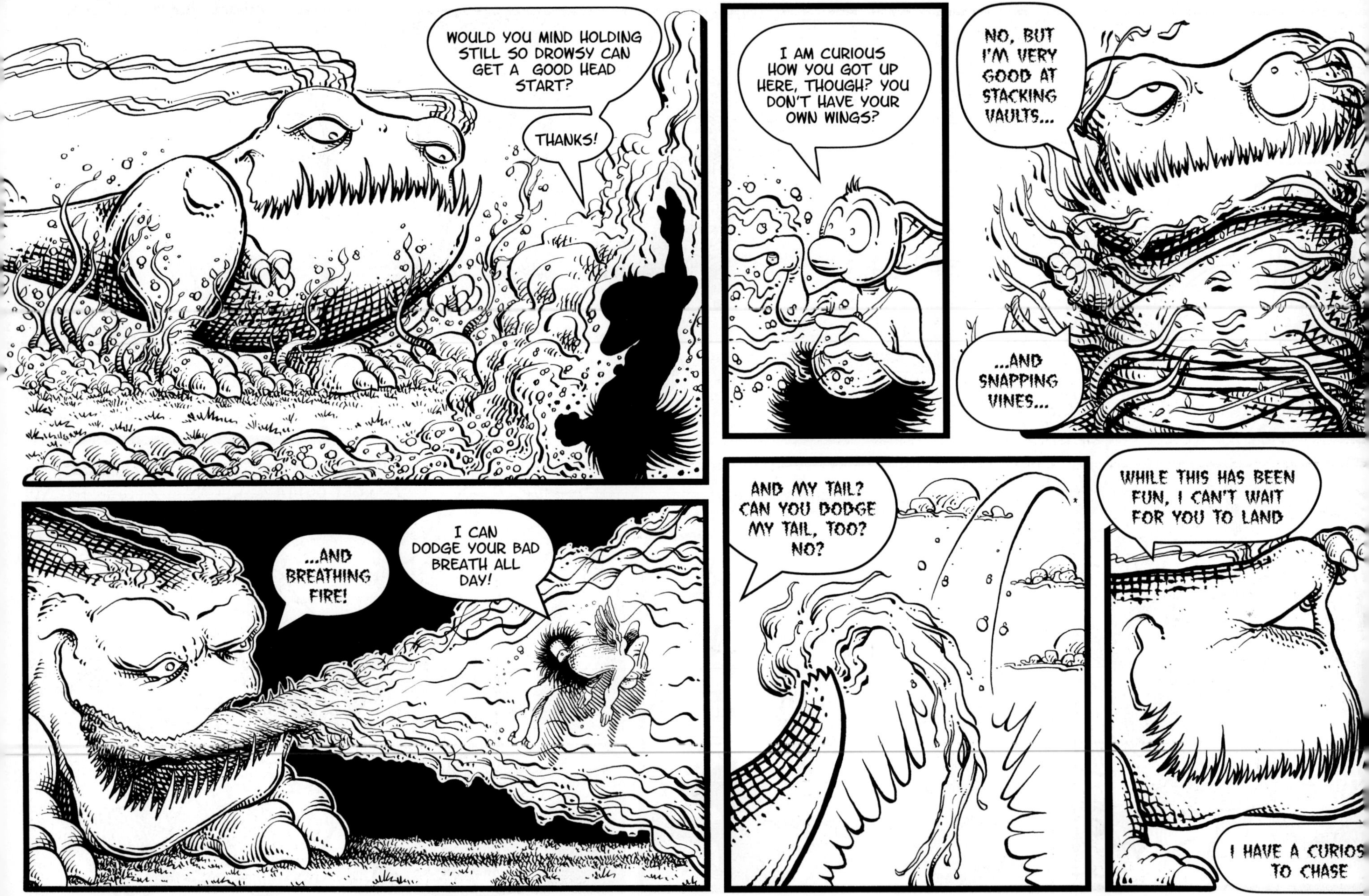
WOULD YOU MIND HOLDING STILL SO DROWSY CAN GET A GOOD HEAD START?
THANKS!
I AM CURIOUS HOW YOU GOT UP HERE, THOUGH? YOU DON'T HAVE YOUR OWN WINGS?
NO, BUT I'M VERY GOOD AT STACKING VAULTS...
...AND SNAPPING VINES...
...AND BREATHING FIRE!
I CAN DODGE YOUR BAD BREATH ALL DAY!
AND MY TAIL? CAN YOU DODGE MY TAIL, TOO? NO?
WHILE THIS HAS BEEN FUN, I CAN'T WAIT FOR YOU TO LAND
I HAVE A CURIOS TO CHASE

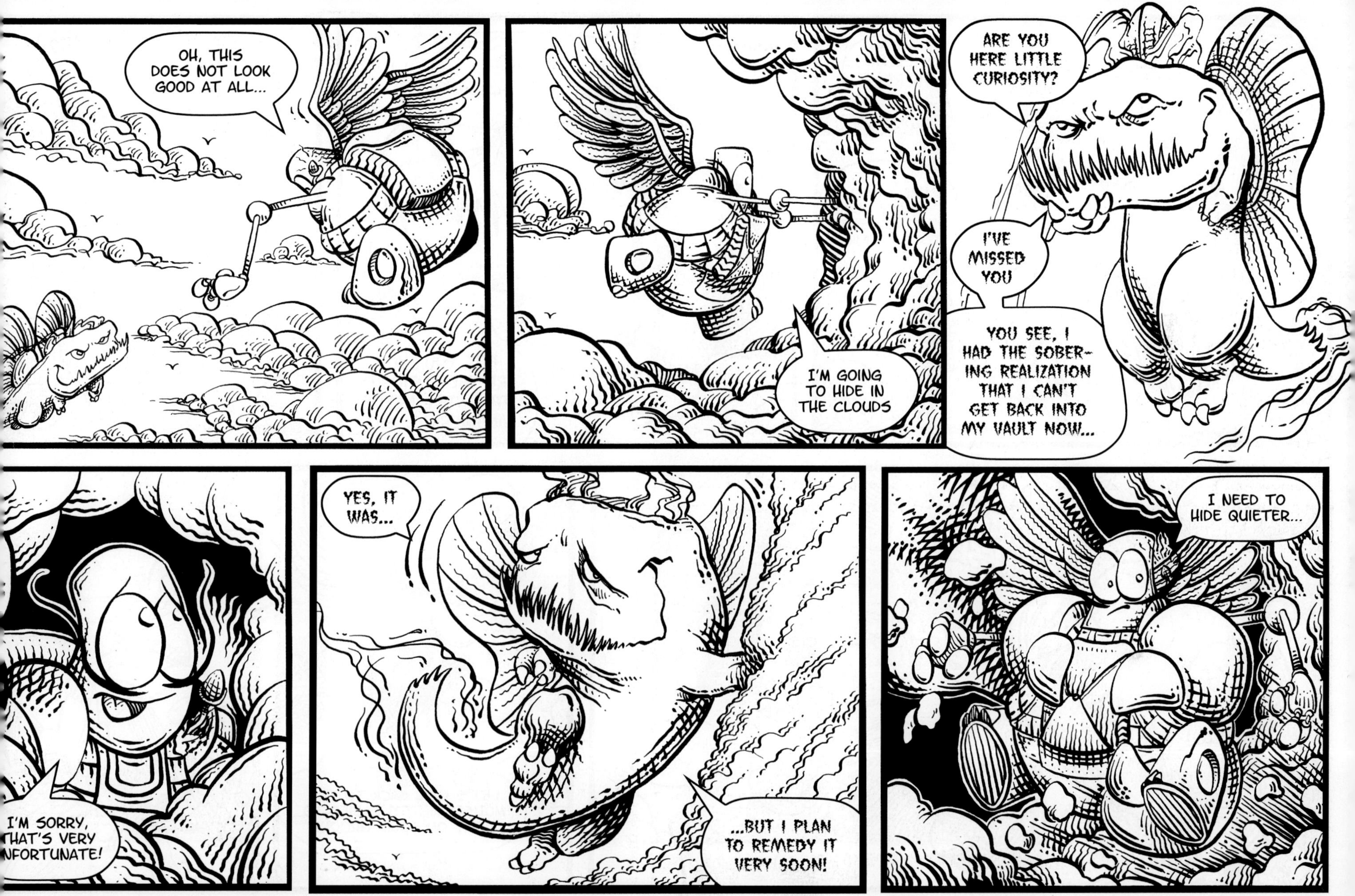
OH, THIS DOES NOT LOOK GOOD AT ALL...
I'M GOING TO HIDE IN THE CLOUDS
ARE YOU HERE LITTLE CURIOSITY?
I'VE MISSED YOU
YOU SEE, I HAD THE SOBER-ING REALIZATION THAT I CAN'T GET BACK INTO MY VAULT NOW...
I'M SORRY, THAT'S VERY NFORTUNATE!
YES, IT WAS...
...BUT I PLAN TO REMEDY IT VERY SOON!
I NEED TO HIDE QUIETER...

HELLO THERE...

HELLO! SO IF YOU'RE HERE, WHAT HAPPENED TO THE TINKS OF ORN?

WHO KNOWS? RAN OFF I EXPECT, BUT I ALREADY KNOW WHAT THEY CONTAIN

BUT YOU...YOU ARE THE CURIOSITY THAT STILL NEEDS ANSWERING...EH?

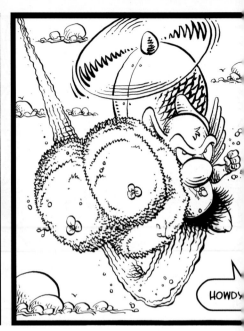

HOWDY

POW! RIGHT IN THE KISSER!

WHY THANK YOU!

YOU OK?

OH SURE, JUST A BIT DIZZY

LET'S FALL BACK TO THE MOUSEION! IT'S EASIER TO FIGHT ON SOLID GROUND

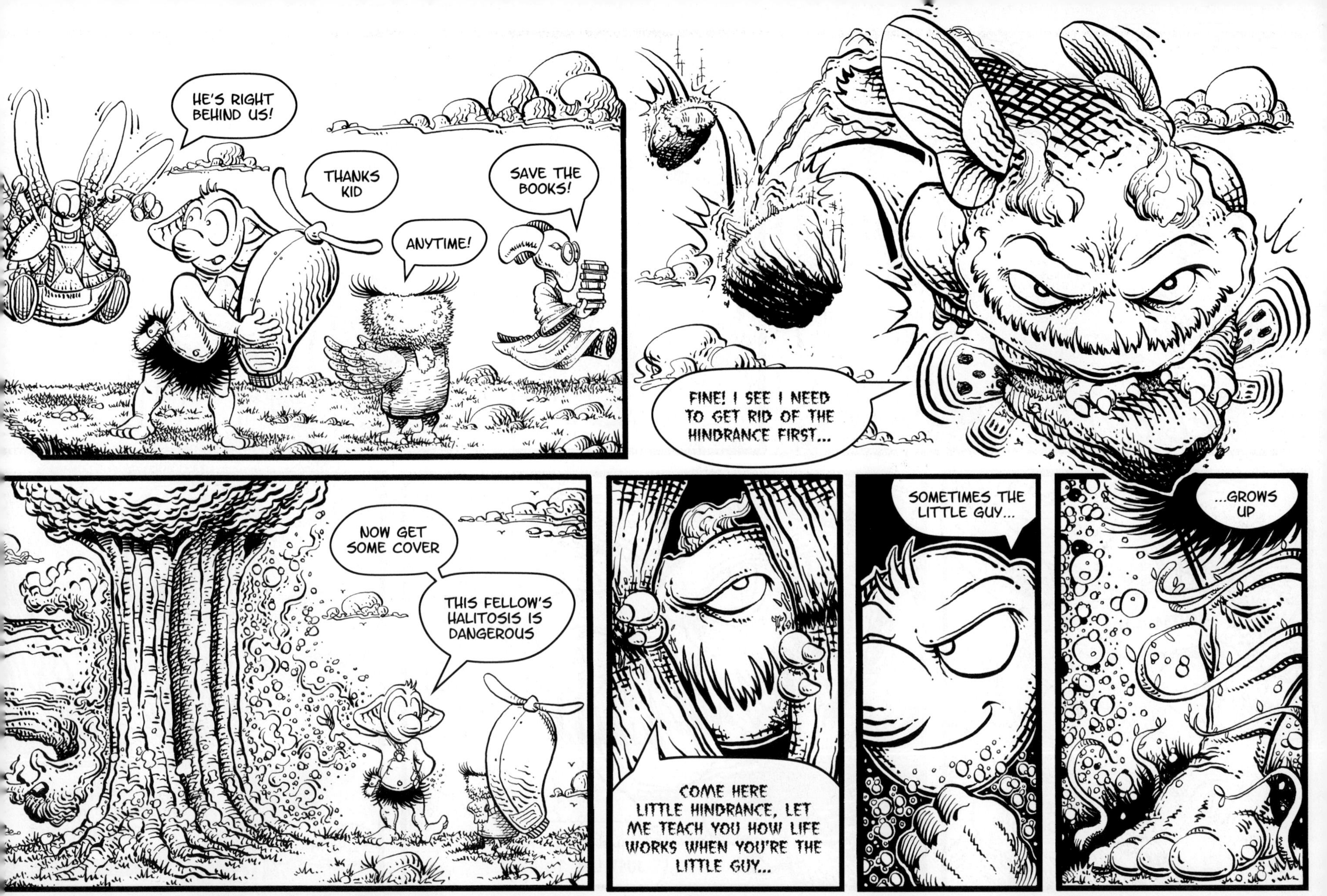
HE'S RIGHT BEHIND US!
THANKS KID
SAVE THE BOOKS!
ANYTIME!
FINE! I SEE I NEED TO GET RID OF THE HINDRANCE FIRST...
NOW GET SOME COVER
THIS FELLOW'S HALITOSIS IS DANGEROUS
COME HERE LITTLE HINDRANCE, LET ME TEACH YOU HOW LIFE WORKS WHEN YOU'RE THE LITTLE GUY...
SOMETIMES THE LITTLE GUY...
...GROWS UP

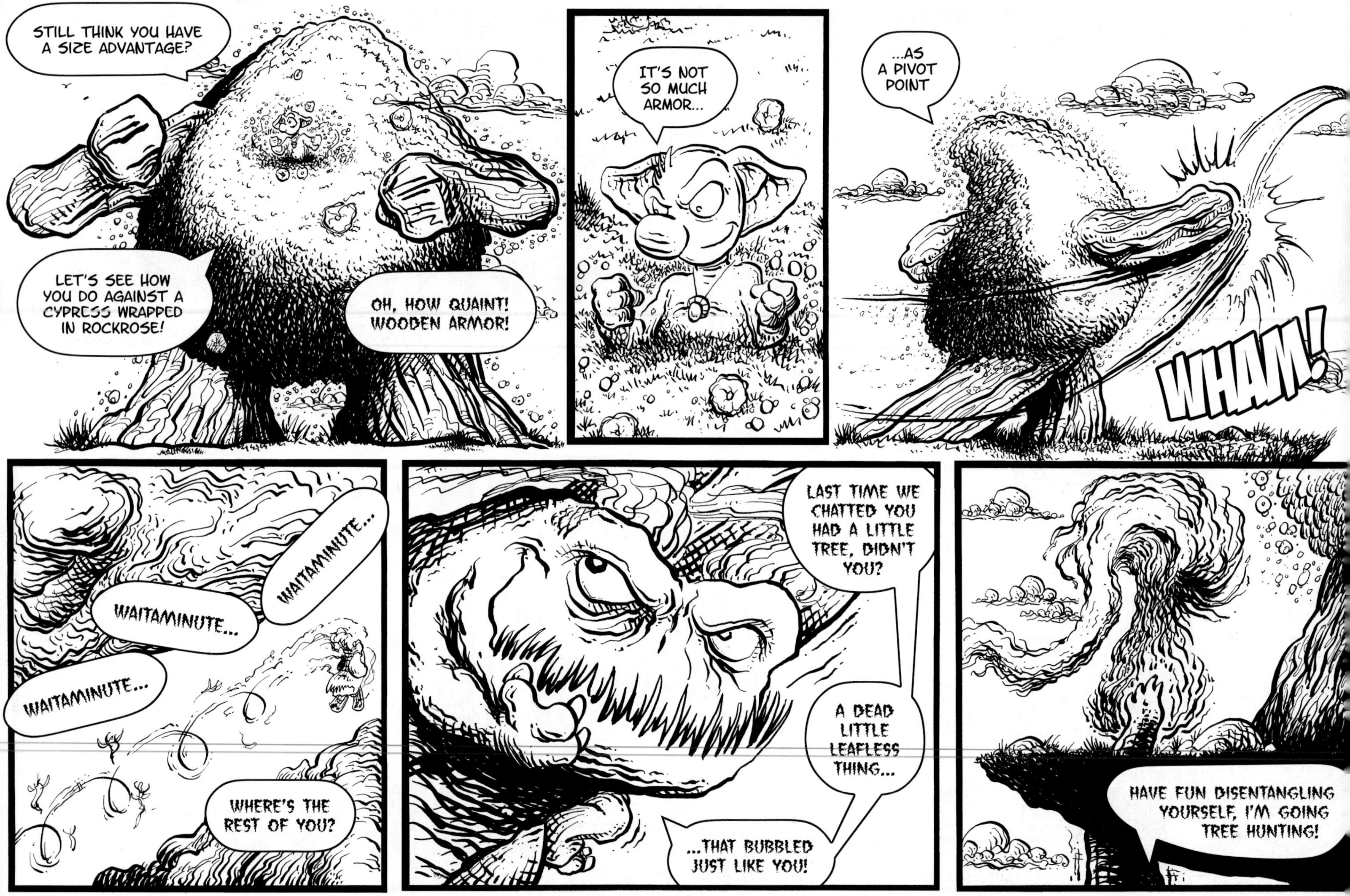
STILL THINK YOU HAVE A SIZE ADVANTAGE?
LET'S SEE HOW YOU DO AGAINST A CYPRESS WRAPPED IN ROCKROSE!
OH, HOW QUAINT! WOODEN ARMOR!
IT'S NOT SO MUCH ARMOR...
...AS A PIVOT POINT
WHAM!
WAITAMINUTE...
WAITAMINUTE...
WAITAMINUTE...
WHERE'S THE REST OF YOU?
LAST TIME WE CHATTED YOU HAD A LITTLE TREE, DIDN'T YOU?
A DEAD LITTLE LEAFLESS THING...
...THAT BUBBLED JUST LIKE YOU!
HAVE FUN DISENTANGLING YOURSELF, I'M GOING TREE HUNTING!

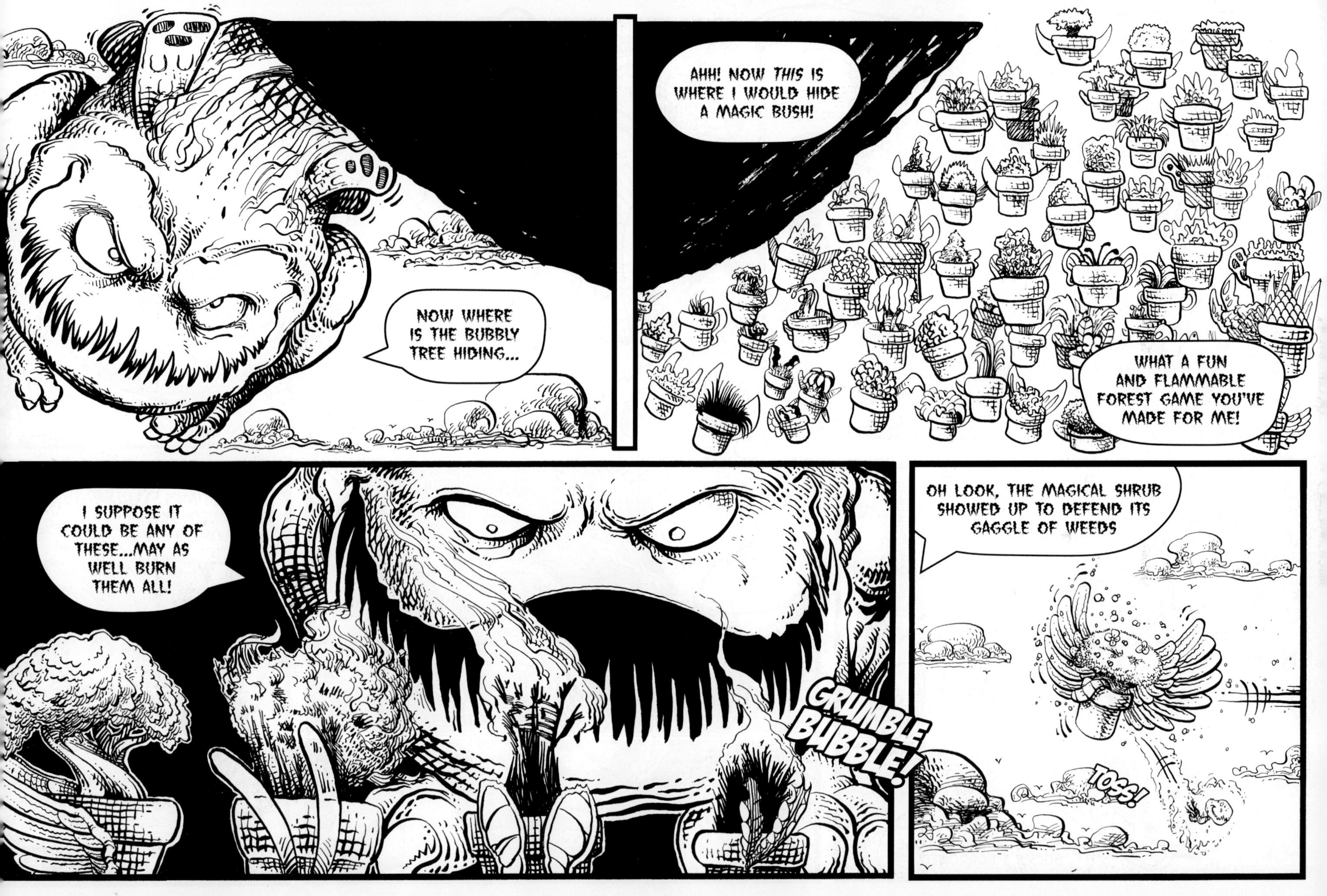
NOW WHERE IS THE BUBBLY TREE HIDING...
AHH! NOW THIS IS WHERE I WOULD HIDE A MAGIC BUSH!
WHAT A FUN AND FLAMMABLE FOREST GAME YOU'VE MADE FOR ME!
I SUPPOSE IT COULD BE ANY OF THESE...MAY AS WELL BURN THEM ALL!
GRUMBLE BUBBLE!
OH LOOK, THE MAGICAL SHRUB SHOWED UP TO DEFEND ITS GAGGLE OF WEEDS
TOSS!

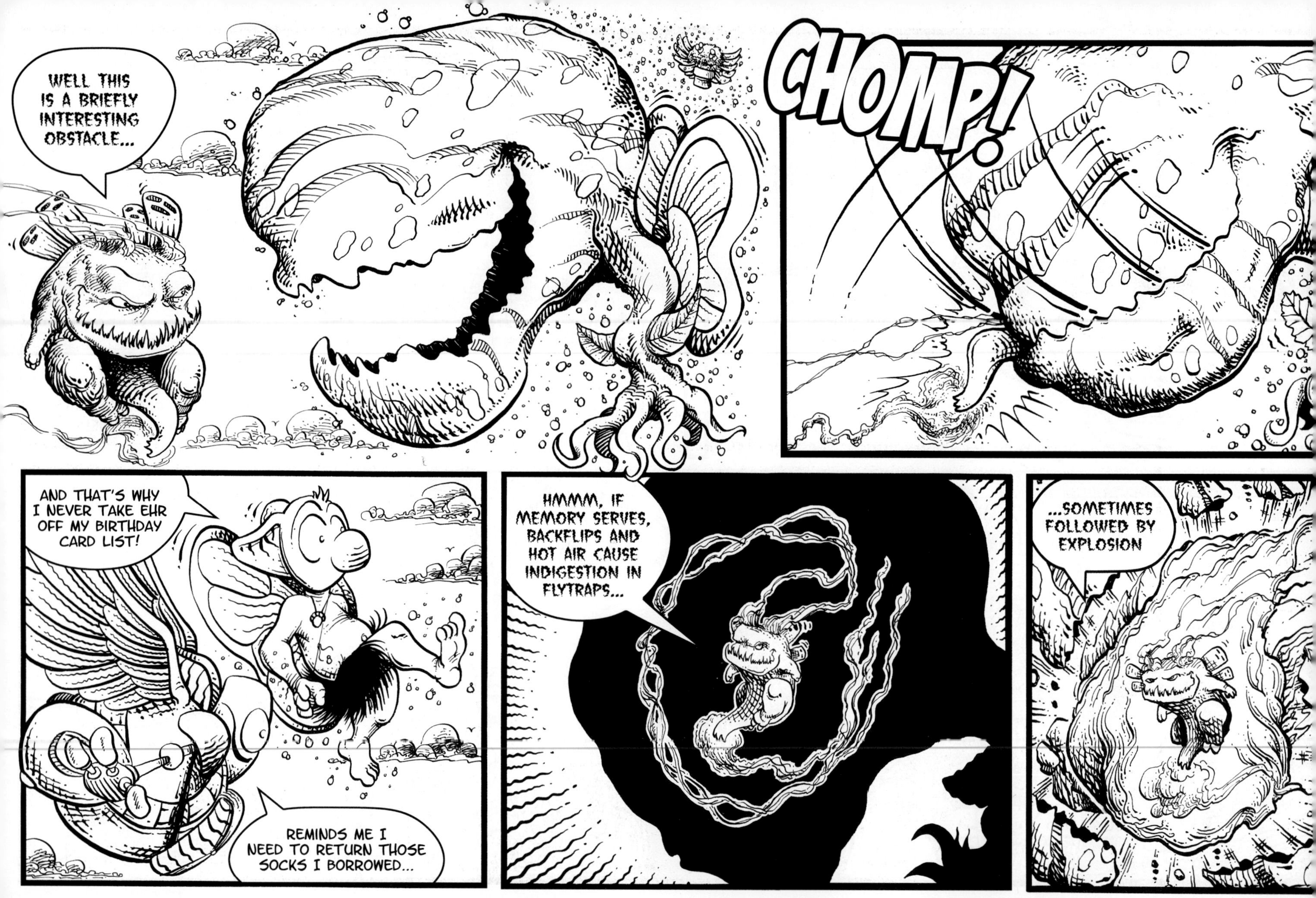
WELL THIS IS A BRIEFLY INTERESTING OBSTACLE...
CHOMP!
AND THAT'S WHY I NEVER TAKE EHR OFF MY BIRTHDAY CARD LIST!
REMINDS ME I NEED TO RETURN THOSE SOCKS I BORROWED...
HMMM, IF MEMORY SERVES, BACKFLIPS AND HOT AIR CAUSE INDIGESTION IN FLYTRAPS...
...SOMETIMES FOLLOWED BY EXPLOSION

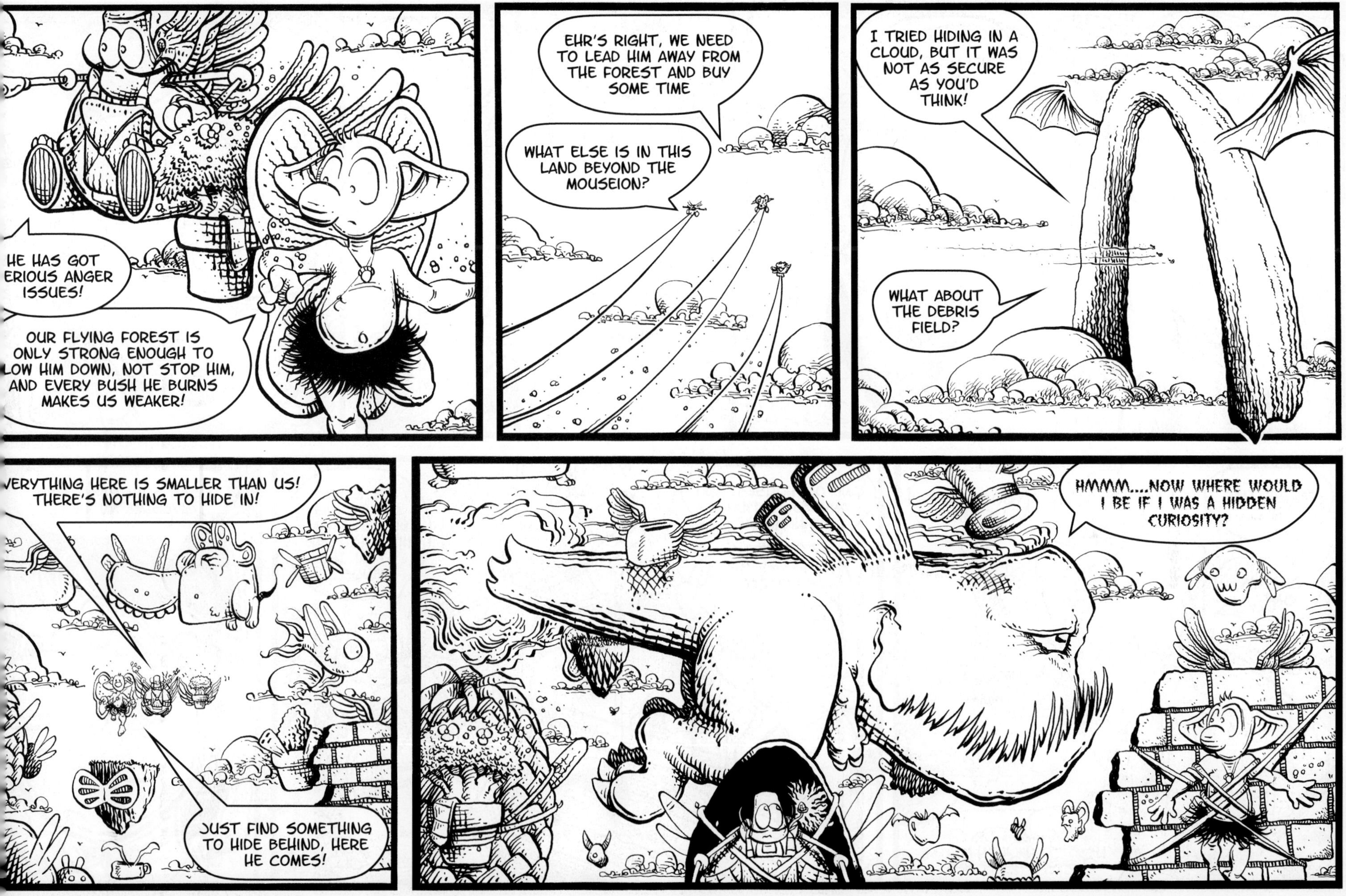
HE HAS GOT ERIOUS ANGER ISSUES!
OUR FLYING FOREST IS ONLY STRONG ENOUGH TO LOW HIM DOWN, NOT STOP HIM, AND EVERY BUSH HE BURNS MAKES US WEAKER!
EHR'S RIGHT, WE NEED TO LEAD HIM AWAY FROM THE FOREST AND BUY SOME TIME
WHAT ELSE IS IN THIS LAND BEYOND THE MOUSEION?
I TRIED HIDING IN A CLOUD, BUT IT WAS NOT AS SECURE AS YOU'D THINK!
WHAT ABOUT THE DEBRIS FIELD?
VERYTHING HERE IS SMALLER THAN US! THERE'S NOTHING TO HIDE IN!
JUST FIND SOMETHING TO HIDE BEHIND, HERE HE COMES!
HMMM....NOW WHERE WOULD I BE IF I WAS A HIDDEN CURIOSITY?

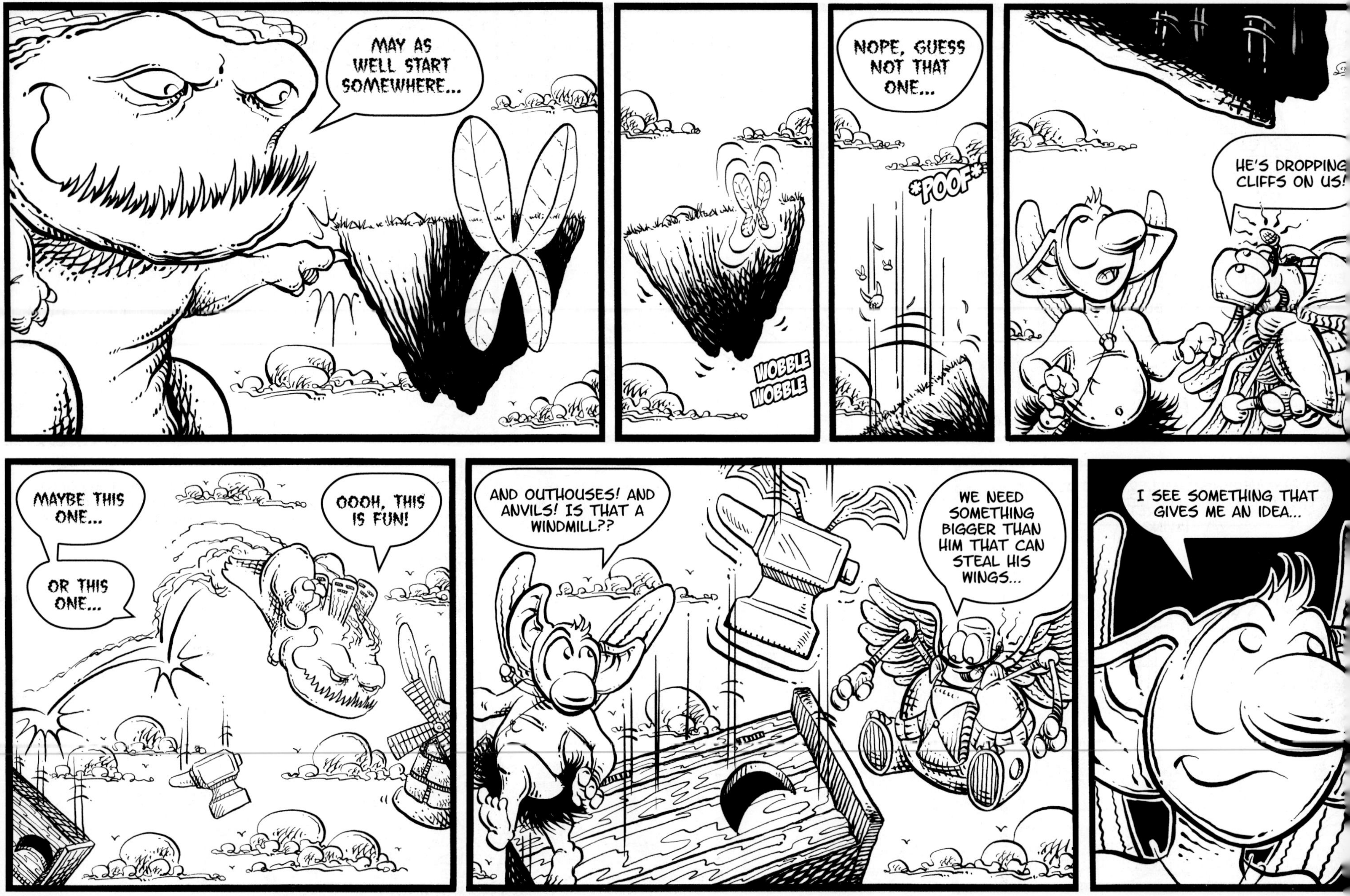
MAY AS WELL START SOMEWHERE...
WOBBLE WOBBLE
NOPE, GUESS NOT THAT ONE...
POOF
HE'S DROPPING CLIFFS ON US!
MAYBE THIS ONE...
OR THIS ONE...
OOOH, THIS IS FUN!
AND OUTHOUSES! AND ANVILS! IS THAT A WINDMILL??
WE NEED SOMETHING BIGGER THAN HIM THAT CAN STEAL HIS WINGS...
I SEE SOMETHING THAT GIVES ME AN IDEA...

BUT FIRST I NEED TO GET THERE...
LOOKS LIKE I SHOOK LOOSE A BEAN!
SADLY FOR YOU, I PREFER MY BEANS BAKED!
GOTCHA!
WHAT, AWW CRUDGE, NOT AGAIN! THAT EAR JUST FINISHED HEALING!
I AM SERIOUSLY REGRETTING NOT HAVING A REPLACEMENT CHUTE NOW...
BUT MAYBE I CAN USE THE MOMENTUM...
...TO PUT SOME DISTANCE BETWEEN US
NOW I HOPE THEY CAN DISTRACT HIM FOR A MINUTE WITHOUT GETTING HURT...

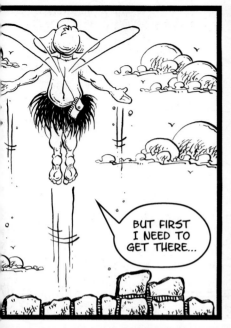

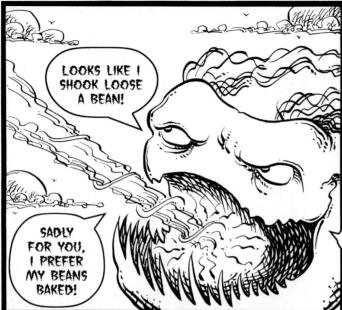

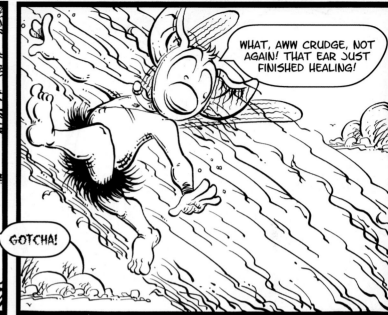

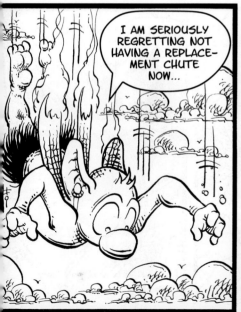

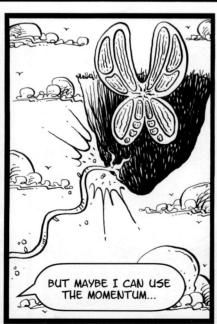

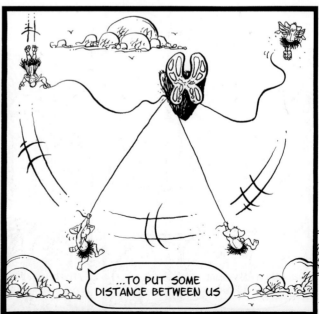

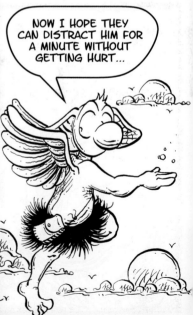

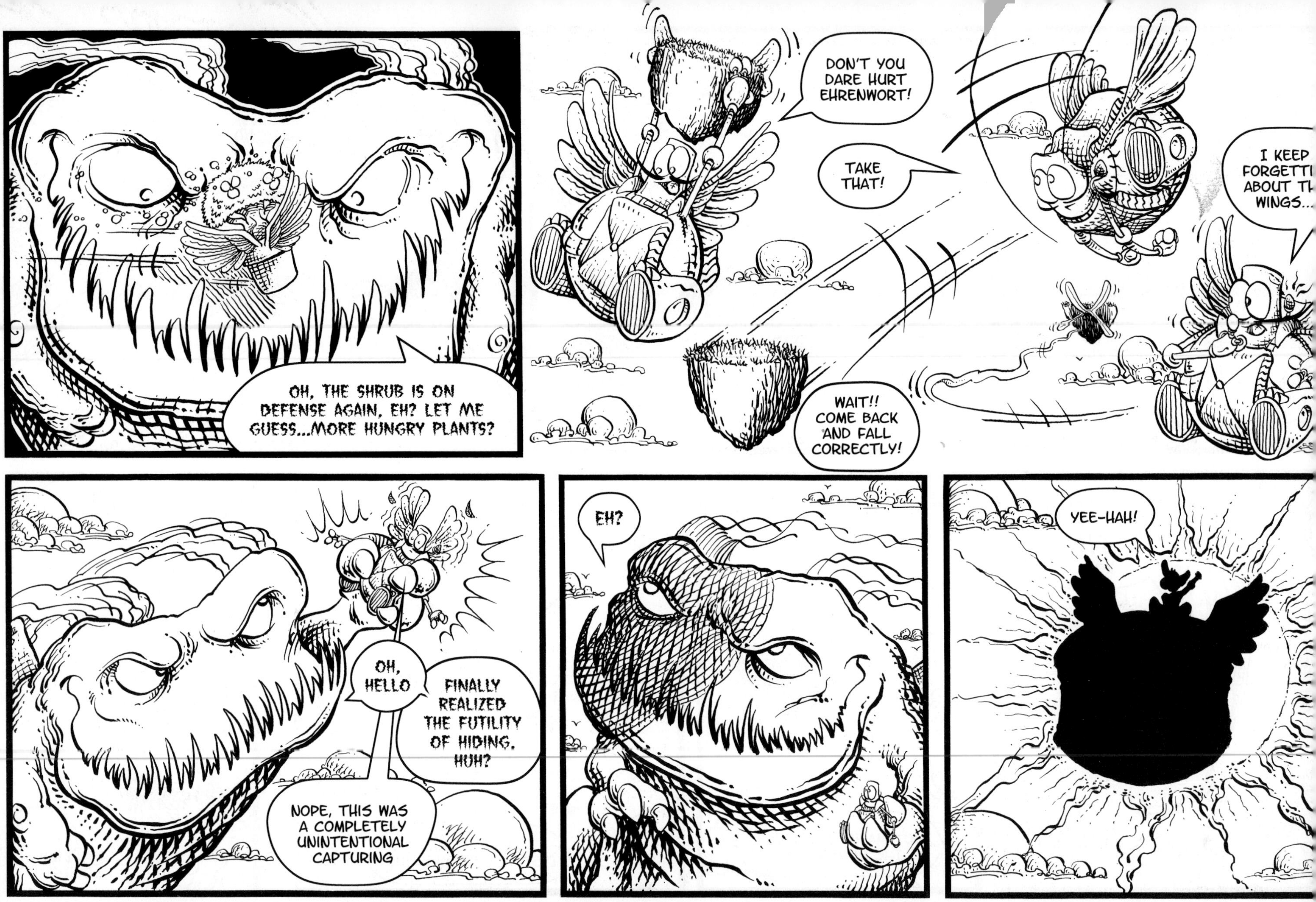
OH, THE SHRUB IS ON DEFENSE AGAIN, EH? LET ME GUESS...MORE HUNGRY PLANTS?
DON'T YOU DARE HURT EHRENWORT!
TAKE THAT!
WAIT!! COME BACK AND FALL CORRECTLY!
I KEEP FORGETTI ABOUT TH WINGS...
FINALLY REALIZED THE FUTILITY OF HIDING, HUH?
OH, HELLO
NOPE, THIS WAS A COMPLETELY UNINTENTIONAL CAPTURING
EH?
YEE-HAH!

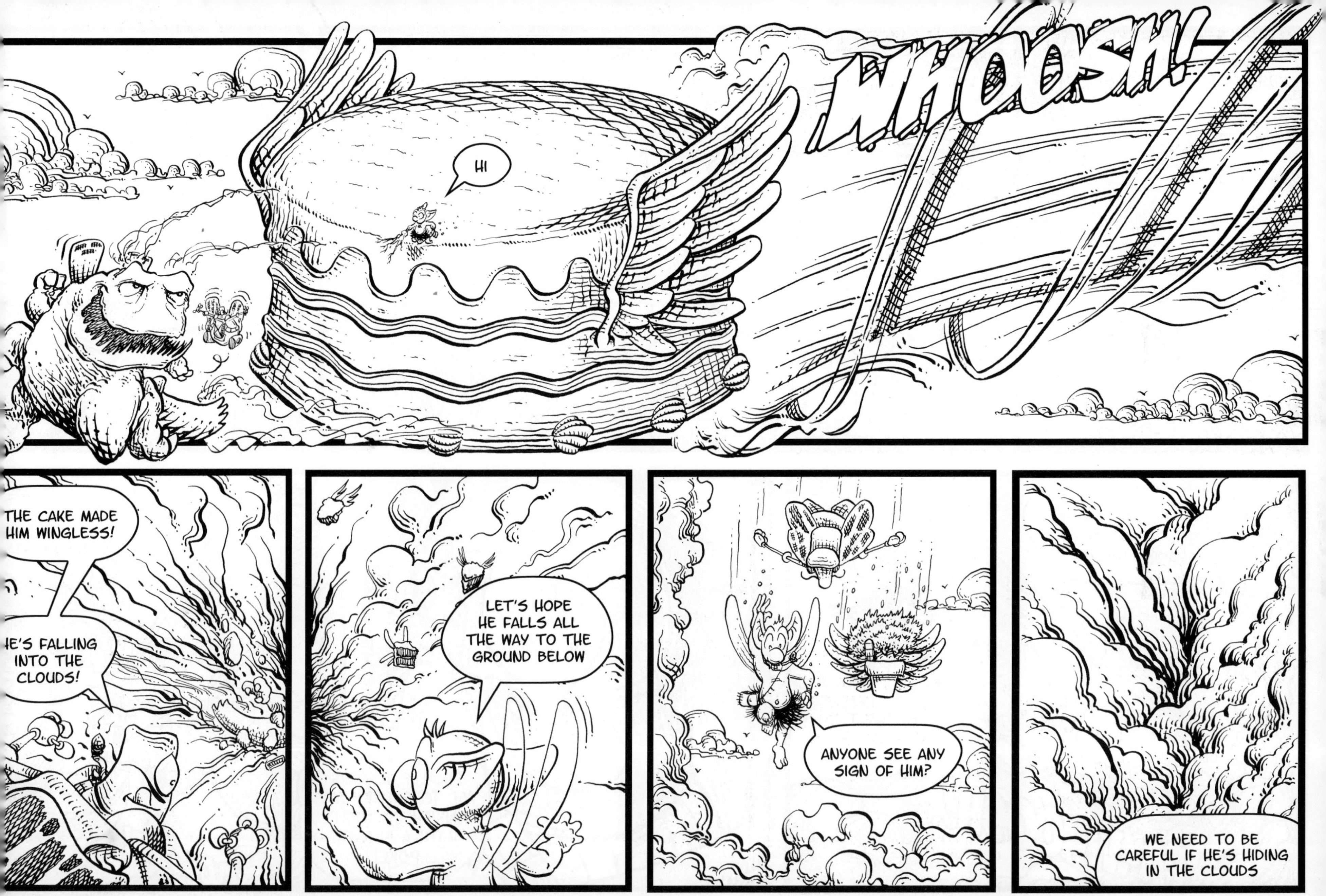
HI
WHOOSH!
THE CAKE MADE HIM WINGLESS!
HE'S FALLING INTO THE CLOUDS!
LET'S HOPE HE FALLS ALL THE WAY TO THE GROUND BELOW
ANYONE SEE ANY SIGN OF HIM?
WE NEED TO BE CAREFUL IF HE'S HIDING IN THE CLOUDS

ME? HIDE? WHAT A SPORTING IDEA!
FIRST, WE'LL GET RID OF YOUR LITTLE BUBBLE FACTORY...
WHAM!
EHRENWORT!!!
THEN I'LL TORCH YOU AND YOUR LITTLE FAERIE WINGS
FA-WHOOSH!
FARLAINE!
WHICH FINALLY ALLOWS ME TO SATISFY MY TINKISH CURIOSITY WITH A FINGER POKE!
HEY! THAT'S GIVIN ME A BELLY ACHE!
CLONG-RIP!

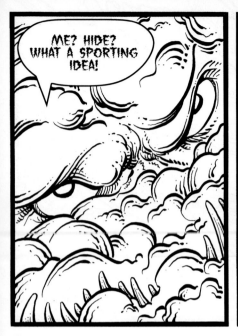

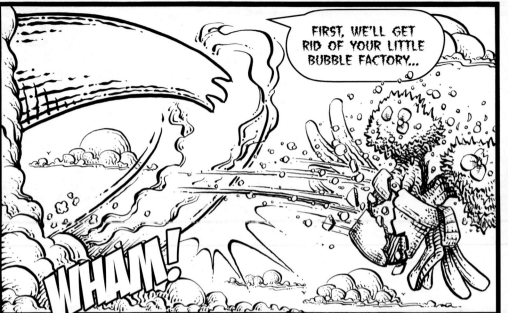

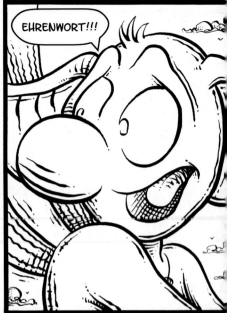

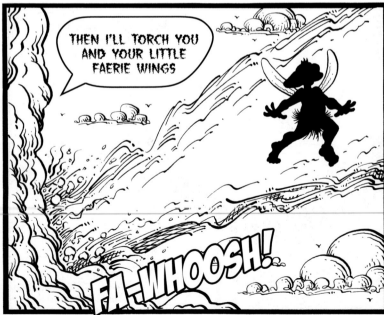

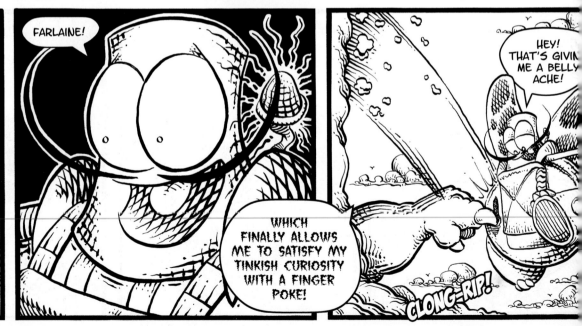

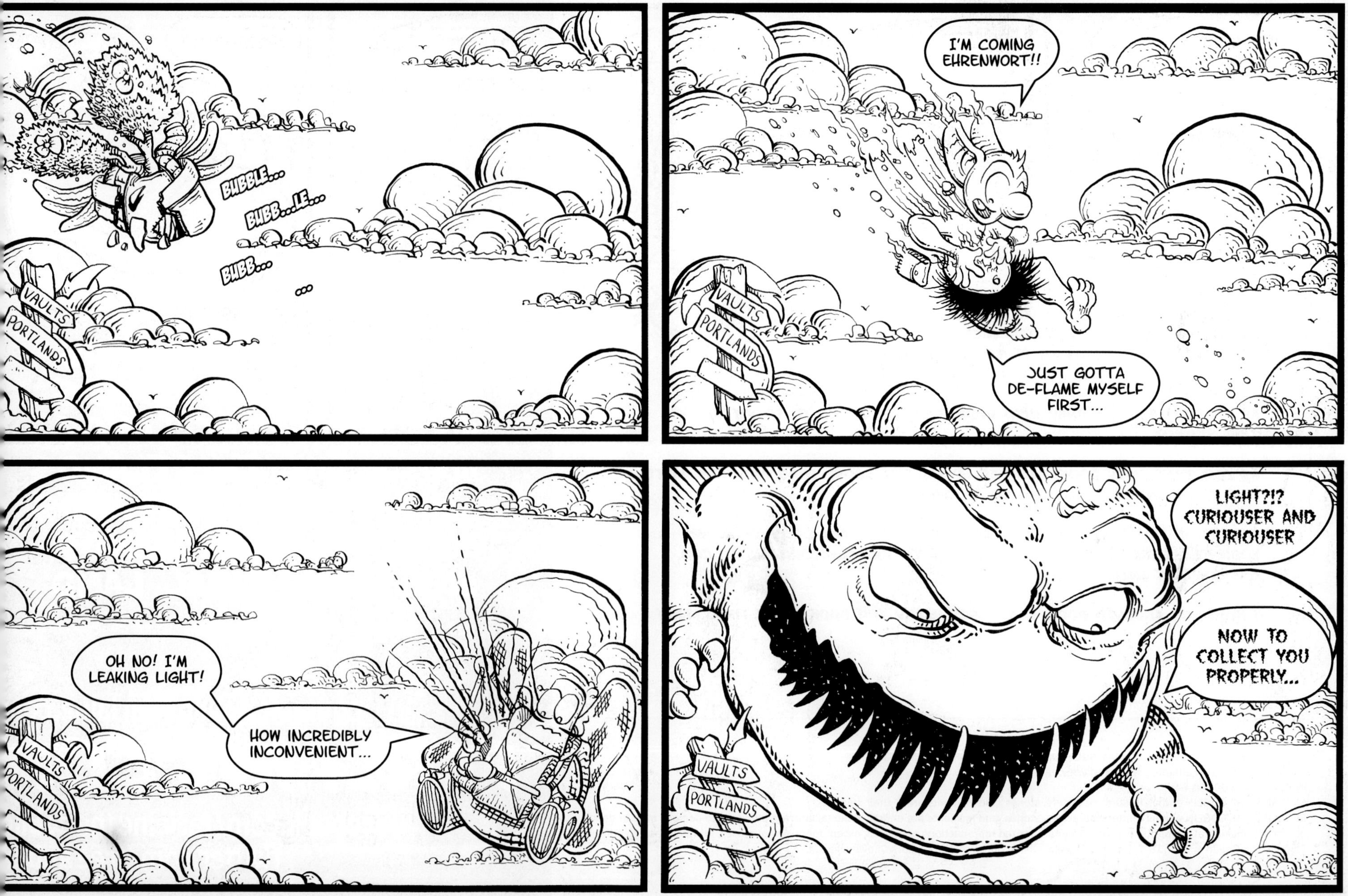
BUBBLE...
BUBB...LE...
BUBB...
...
VAULTS
PORTLANDS
I'M COMING EHRENWORT!!
JUST GOTTA DE-FLAME MYSELF FIRST...
VAULTS
PORTLANDS
OH NO! I'M LEAKING LIGHT!
HOW INCREDIBLY INCONVENIENT...
VAULTS
PORTLANDS
LIGHT?!? CURIOUSER AND CURIOUSER
NOW TO COLLECT YOU PROPERLY...
VAULTS
PORTLANDS

CONTINUED IN BOOK 7: THE FINAL LAND

MARCH 2018

HOWDY GANG!

THE SECOND TO LAST BOOK!

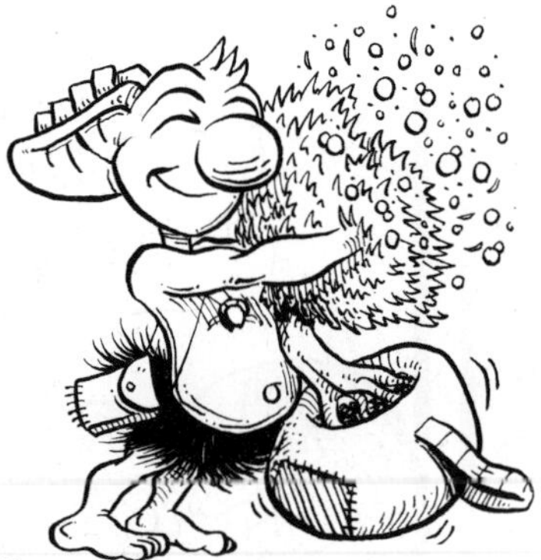

AS USUAL, I'M A BIT BEHIND MY GOAL, BUT IT'S NOT AS BAD AS IT LOOKS!

I FINISHED BOOK 6 IN OCTOBER, BUT BECAUSE I KNEW BOOK 7 WOULD DOVETAIL NICELY, I TRIED TO HOLD OFF ON RELEASING IT SO BOOKS 6-7 CAME OUT CLOSER TOGETHER.

AS I TYPE THIS I'M MIDWAY INTO BOOK 7 AND PLAN FOR IT TO HIT SHELVES THIS SUMMER.

AS FOR THAT FINAL BOOK, I'VE TIED UP ALL THE LOOSE ENDS AND HOPE YOU'LL FIND IT AN ENTERTAINING AND SOLID CLIMAX!

FINALLY, IF ANYONE WAS INTERESTED IN OWNING A PAGE OF ORIGINAL ART FROM THE SERIES, I'VE GIVEN SOME PAGES TO WWW.COMICORIGINALART.COM. (OR CONTACT ME!)

I HOPE YOU ENJOYED BOOK 6, AND GET READY FOR BOOK 7: THE FINAL LAND!

- PUG

FARLAINE THE GOBLIN. Book 6, THE WINGLANDS, March 2018 FIRST PRINTING.
Published by Studio Farlaine, goblin@farlaine.com
ISBN 978-0-9890058-6-9

Written and Drawn by Pug Grumble
Cover Colors by Jean-Francois Beaulieu
Variant Cover by Larry MacDougall

READ ALL OF FARLAINE'S ADVENTURES!

BOOK 1: THE TINKLANDS
BOOK 2: THE SALTLANDS
BOOK 3: THE RACELANDS
BOOK 4: THE TWISTLANDS
BOOK 5: THE VAULTLANDS
BOOK 6: THE WINGLANDS
BOOK 7: THE FINAL LAND

contact: goblin@farlaine.com

FARLAINE.COM

facebook.com/farlainethegoblin
twitter.com/treegoblin

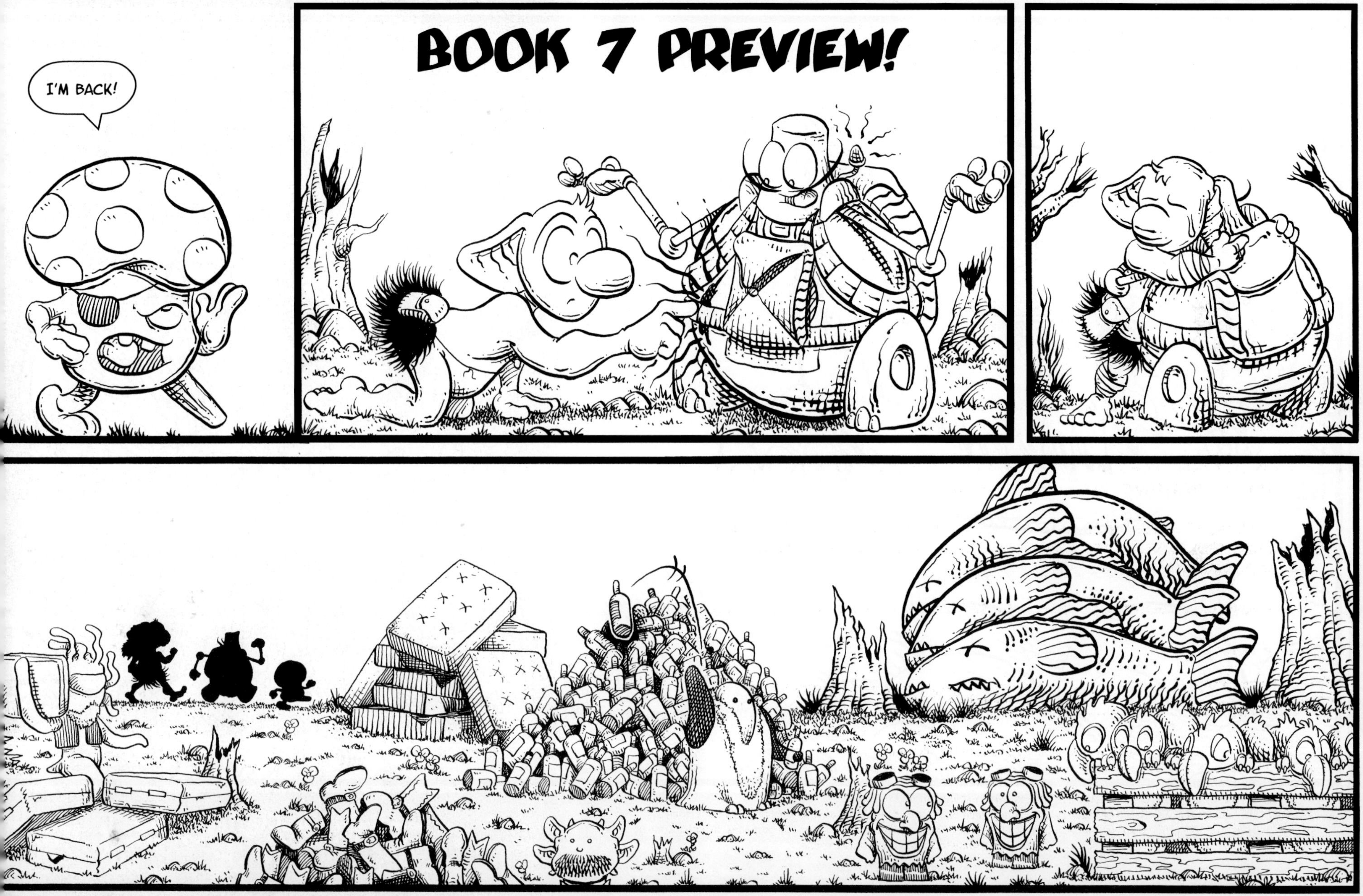
I'M BACK!
BOOK 7 PREVIEW!

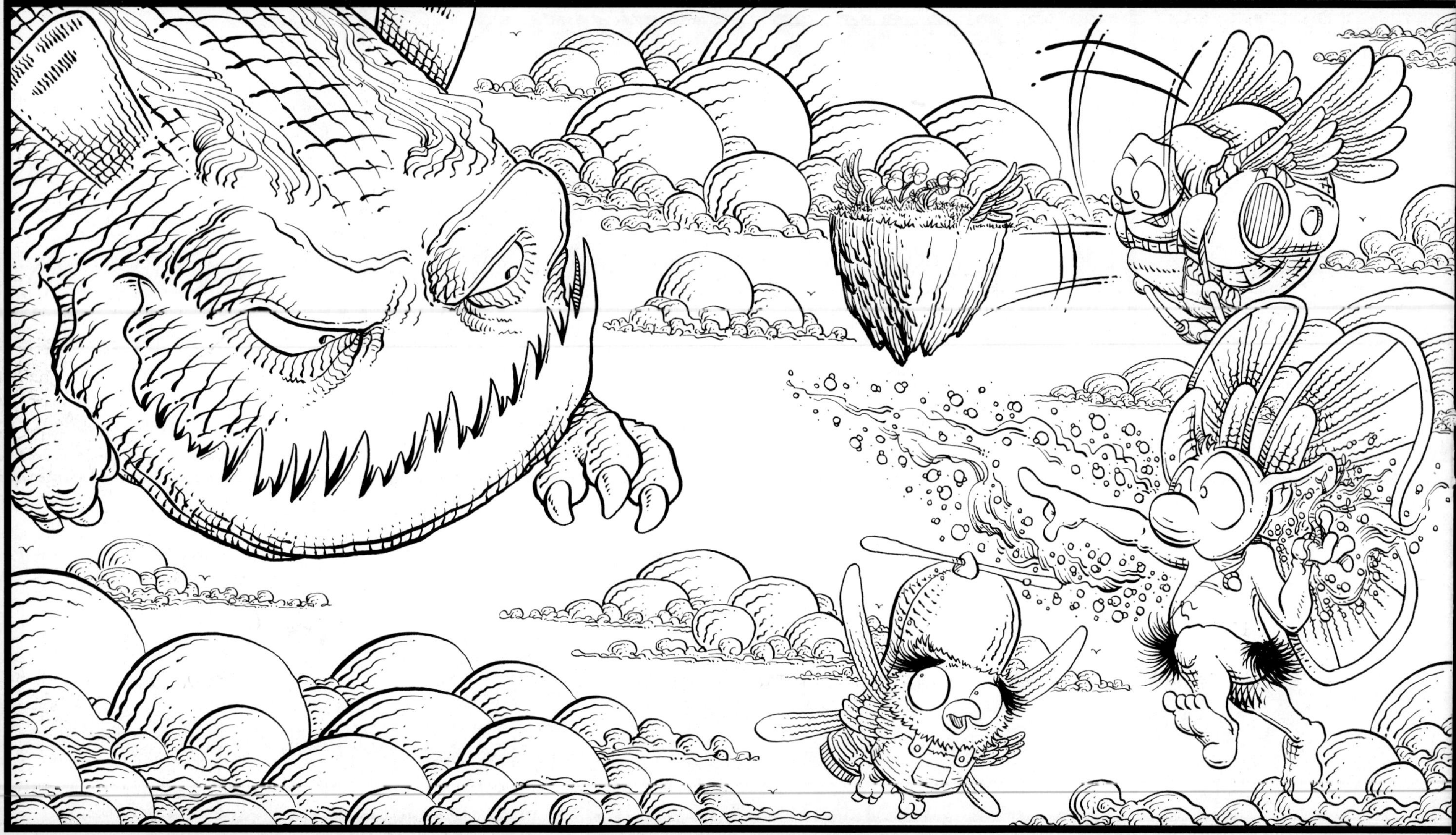

COVER #6 - BLACK + WHITE

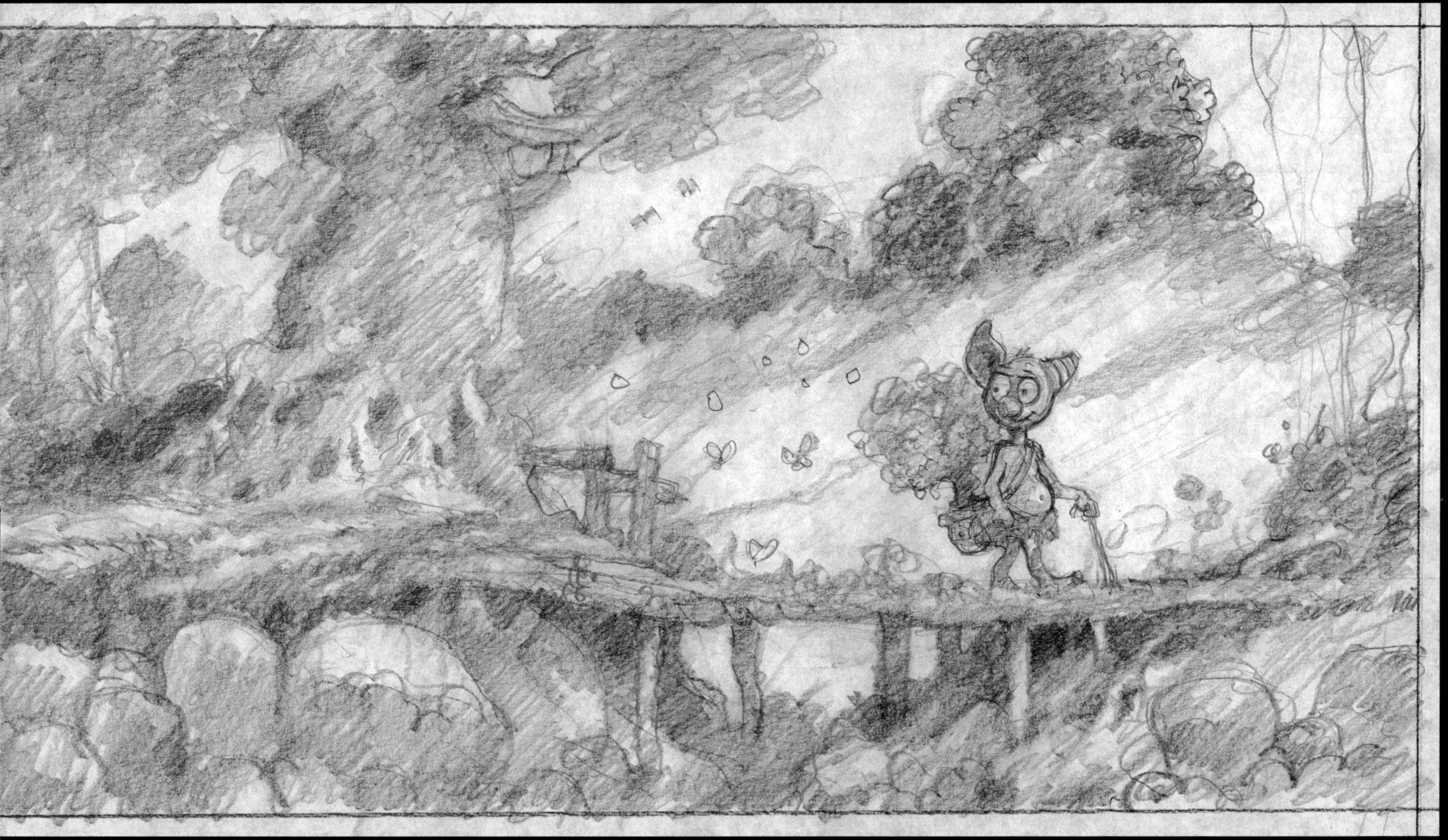

ALTERNATE COVER BY LARRY MACDOUGALL
(THE PAINTED VERSION LOOKS WAY BETTER!)

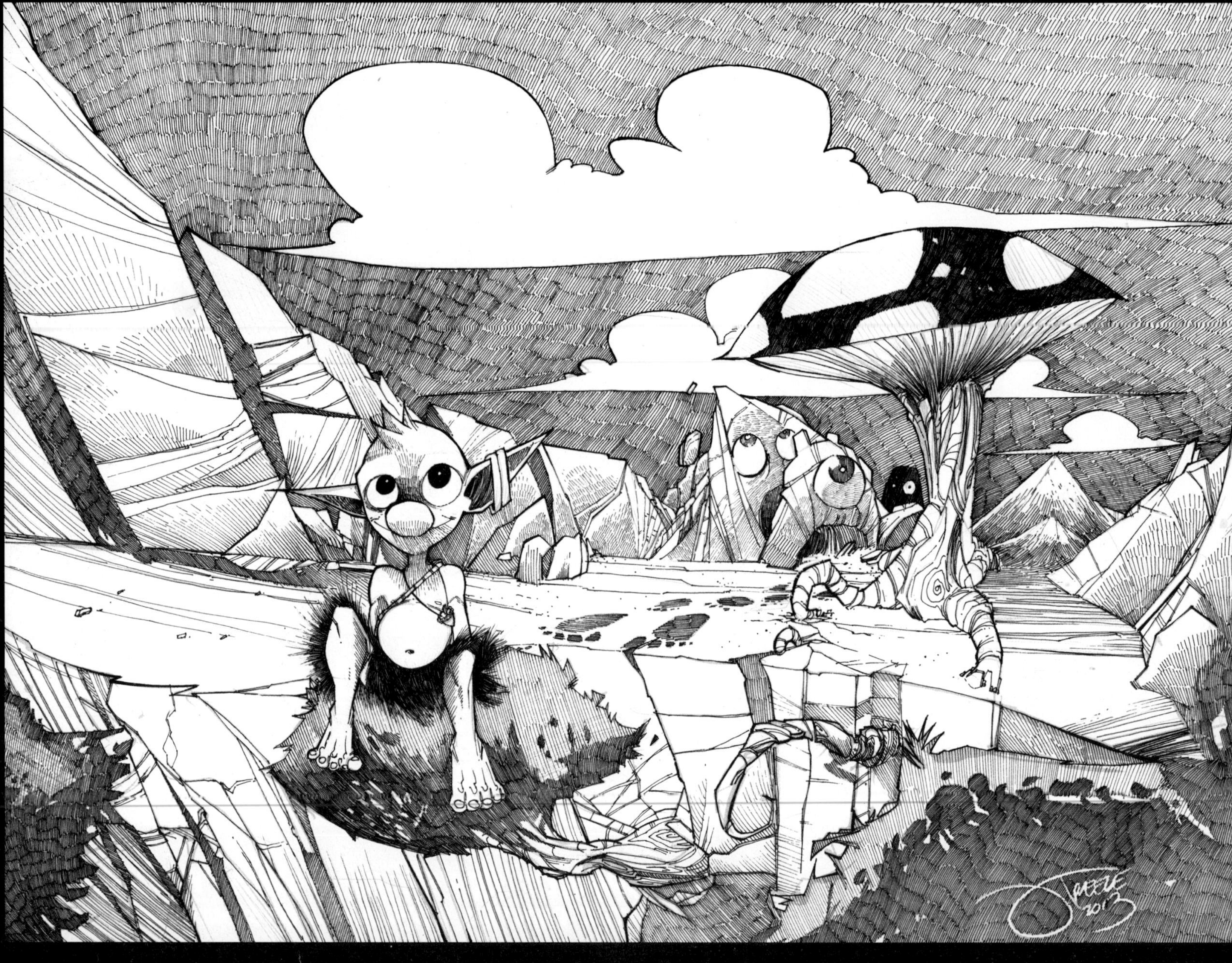
TREECE 2013

PINUP BY JEREMY TREECE